THE MIRACLE OF

BRASSTOWN VALLEY

Stroud & Hall Publishers
P.O. Box 27210
Macon, Ga 31221
www.stroudhall.com

©2007 Stroud & Hall

The paper used in this publication meets the minimum requirements
of American National Standard for Information Sciences—
Permanence of Paper for Printed Library Materials.
ANSI Z39.48–1984. (alk. paper)

Library of Congress Cataloging-in-Publication Data

Miller, Zell, 1932–
The miracle of Brasstown Valley / by Zell Miller.
p. cm.
ISBN 978-0-9796462-0-1 (paperback : alk. paper)
1. Young Harris College—History. 2. Union County (Ga.)—History.
I. Title.

LD6372.M55 2007
378.758'285—dc22
                    2007022971

The Miracle of
Brasstown Valley

Zell Miller

OTHER BOOKS

BY ZELL MILLER

The Mountains Within Me (1975)

Great Georgians (1983)

They Heard Georgia Singing (1985)

Corps Values (1997)

A National Party No More (2003)

A Deficit of Decency (2004)

Contents

About the Cover

Double Knob is a mountain that towers above Brasstown Valley and the village of Young Harris, Georgia.

Birdie Bryan Miller painted the original plate in 1934. She was an art teacher at Young Harris College.

The scene is especially meaningful to the author, for it was here in 1932 that the recent widow waded this creek and gathered beautiful stones to build a home for her children, Jane and Zell.

Foreword

For three-quarters of a century I have lived with these stories, some of them embellished over the years, about the mountains, the people, their ways, and the birth of a college in Brasstown Valley.

Before I was school aged, my mother had convinced me that Judge Harris was an angel who hovered over the infant school when it was still in swaddling clothes, giving generously and providing the credibility the isolated mountain school needed to an outside world. And Dr. Joe Sharp was the Moses who led the school out of the wilderness to the promised land.

The Reverend Artemas Lester was more of an enigma. An itinerant Methodist preacher, he rode into Brasstown Valley on a mule, started a school, and then left before a single class was held—never to return. In a letter written more than twenty-five years ago, his late grandson, then a doctor at Emory University Hospital, used the word "plodding" to describe his life. I prefer "dogged," and I found that this was the great strength of Reverend Artemas Lester. He was the "squeaking wheel" who through patience, prayer, and persistence got the "grease."

The storyline of this book is about the miracle in Brasstown Valley, Young Harris College, that managed not only to survive through storm and strife but to touch thousands of lives in a positive and profound way—including my own.

But it is much more than that because I also write about that mystical valley, Choestoe in Union County, "where the rabbits dance" and where, even in the 1880s, education was exalted. I write of these oldest mountains in the world where the nation's first "gold rush" occurred, where the fascinating Cherokees lived and suffered a terrible tragedy. I write of the shrewd, spunky, and spirited settlers of this once isolated frontier and their vanishing ways.

While all the people, places, and most events are real, in some instances I have filtered their undocumented words spoken long ago through my imagination. So be forewarned: this history is not pure and perfect; it's padded. But, as we say in the mountains, this is "pert near" how it all happened.

—Zell Miller
May 2007

With love and appreciation this book is dedicated to two Young Harris College Presidents much like Dr. Joseph A. Sharp:

Dr. Charles R. Clegg and Fay (1950–1967)

Dr. T. Jackson Lance and Annie Rose
(1932–1942)

"A man's heart plans his way, but God directs his steps."

Proverbs 16:9

CHAPTER 1

The Call

Knife-blade thin, the Reverend Milford G. Hamby of Union County stood well over six feet tall. His piercing eyes could look straight into your soul. His deep mountain twang could rattle even the back row of the small Methodist church in Yatesville, Georgia. His towering presence could turn the disbelievers into the devout, the sinner into the saved, and the lawless frontier into a civilized society.

A young man named Artemas Lester was mesmerized by the soaring oratory of this exhorter from the mountains. The call had been gnawing at Artemas for sometime now. Not long after his mother had died, leaving him at fourteen the oldest of seven sons, responsibility had rested heavily on his narrow shoulders. That was when he had begun to attend church seriously without any urging from anyone and even brought several of his brothers with him.

The Reverend Hamby was bringing his sermon to its soul-shattering climax; the invitation would be next. Artemas knew that this time he would not hang back as he had done so many times in the past after hearing other preachers, for days afterward regretting it. This time, he would follow his heart, go forward, and accept the Lord Jesus Christ as his Savior.

But it was more than just accepting Christ; he had done that in his heart years ago. He wanted what the Reverend Hamby had. He wanted to preach the gospel and save souls himself. He wanted to join the ranks of a circuit rider just like Hamby who, from the age of nineteen, traveled all over North Georgia on horseback much like Francis Asbury had done in America decades before and as Charles and John Wesley had done before him in England.

Artemas had read of the disappointment both Wesleys experienced when they came to the colony of Georgia with General James

Oglethorpe a century and a half earlier. The son of a wealthy British aristocrat, Oglethorpe had forsaken personal pleasure for public service. As a member of Parliament, he became interested in the plight of those thrown into prison for small debts their squalid, hopeless lives could not avoid. He dreamed of establishing a colony in the New World where free and equal men, through their own labors, could build self-sufficient lives for themselves and their families.

In 1733, Oglethorpe personally led a hardy band of 114 hand-picked colonists—none of them debtors—in establishing the settlement of Savannah, and he laid out the picturesque squares that characterize the great city. He personally cemented the ties of friend-ship with Chief Tomochichi and neighboring Indian tribes. Later he brought the two young Wesley brothers with him to this new, thir-teenth British colony of Georgia. Charles was his personal secretary, and John planned to minister to the Indians. Oglethorpe even person-ally commanded the troops who defeated the advancing Spanish in the Battle of Bloody Marsh on St. Simons Island, saving the English colonies to the north of Georgia. For a while at least, he personally kept whiskey, lawyers, and slavery out of his new colony.

As the Reverend Hamby came down out of the pulpit, Artemas knew what he must do, what he was being called to do. "Oh, who will come and go with me? I am bound for the promised land. Are you?" The preacher's voice now was lowered almost to a whisper. "Don't put this off. It's the most important decision you will ever make." Then he quoted John 3:16, a Bible verse Artemas knew well and that gave him great comfort: "'For God so loved the world that he gave his only begotten Son, that whosoever believeth in Him shall not perish but have ever-lasting life.' He wants you, the lost sinner."

Without looking at the Bible he held, Hamby repeated the famil-iar parable: "What man of you, having a hundred sheep, if he loses one of them, doth not leave the ninety and nine in the wilderness, and go after that which is lost, until he finds it? And when he hath found it, he layeth it on his shoulders, rejoicing. And when he cometh home, he calleth together his friends and neighbors, saying unto them, 'Rejoice with me for I have found my sheep which was lost.' I say unto you that likewise joy shall be in heaven over one sinner that repenteth, more than ninety and nine just persons, which need no repentance."

Hamby continued, "Are you that lost sheep? Are you that sinner who can bring joy to heaven, your loved ones, and yourself by repenting? Folks, the Lord brings back his own. Are you that lost sheep who has gone astray? Well, the Lord has found you right here in Yatesville, Georgia. You've been found today, August 15, 1883. Tonight is the night. You can be saved by the grace of God. You can be born again. Do it publicly as Jesus wishes. Do it tonight. Do it now while the choir sings our invitation hymn." Beads of sweat covered the face of the visiting revivalist. He stood straight as an arrow with his arms outstretched.

Softly the voices were raised: "In the cross, in the cross, be my glory ever, 'til my raptured soul shall find rest beyond the river." A middleaged woman went forward, embraced the preacher, and then slowly kneeled at the altar. A man dressed in overalls, a local farmer, was close behind. A teenage girl, her face glistening with tears, was next. And then, almost at a trot, came Artemas Lester with a calm and determined look on his face. The slight twenty-six-year-old, his burden lifted, sank to his knees, and his body quivered with a visible sigh of relief as he tightly interlocked his fingers in prayer. Just as John Wesley had once said of himself, the heart of Artemas Lester was "strangely warmed."

This life-altering decision had been a long time coming. From the time his mother had died nearly twelve years earlier, Artemas had struggled to help his father make ends meet during the hard years of Reconstruction after the Civil War. Coping with the problems of six younger brothers had not been easy. He had felt the duty of his circumstance and had met it every day with an inbred sense of responsibility. Seeing that one was fed and dressed, he would go down the line tending to each in order of their age. From one to another, that is how he had so far spent his life. But sometimes deep down there would be a strong inner feeling that he was destined to do something more in the world beyond Upson and Monroe counties and beyond the Lester family. The boys had now grown into men; even the youngest teenager was bigger than Artemas. He continued to feel the closeness of the Lord, and he had communicated with God on a daily basis for several years and felt that God had something in store for him beyond his present dreary existence. Exactly what, he had no idea.

But it would be something that would last long after he was gone. Something that involved new places, new people, the betterment of other children like his brothers. At first he thought his calling was to be a teacher. He had been a good student, and his grandfather on his mother's side, Donald McDonald, had been a teacher. In fact, Mr. McDonald had a sizable personal library in Yatesville, and Artemas had spent much time there educating himself. He had read every one of his grandfather's books, and some had not been easy.

Artemas knew that sometimes he could be one way, uncompromising, too hot-tempered, outspoken, and impatient. He knew God had given him a good mind and that he had a talent for persuasion. He also knew he had a lot to learn. He read avidly, loved history, and devoured the rare newspapers and magazines he was able to get his hand on from time to time. He might be "book smart" as his father called it, but he had experienced hardly anything of practical value in the busy world he knew was out there.

Exactly when he began to think of the ministry, Artemas was not sure. He loved church services and Sunday school. One of his weekly duties was to get all his brothers ready for church each week, and he could tell Preacher Carter and the elders were impressed when all the Lester family filled an entire bench at the local Methodist church on Sunday morning. When his brothers got into their teens and beyond, they had other things to do and balked at going. Later they would leave home to make their way in the world.

Four were already married and had children of their own. A couple had left the county and gone to Macon and Barnesville. Artemas had remained, helping his father until the smallest could look after themselves. Someday, Artemas thought, he too would leave and see what was out there in this big and diverse state of Georgia. Someday he'd touch lives other than just members of his own family. Someday, Artemas dreamed—no, he *knew*—he'd do something important, something that would last.

But in the middle of these thoughts, Artemas always knew he could not do these great deeds alone. He realized that something or someone bigger than himself would have to help. That was when he knew he had to partner with God, if he ever hoped to make a difference. What was it Isaiah had written? Artemas thought to himself, *To those who have no might, God increases strength.*

All these thoughts came flooding through the mind of Artemas as he kneeled at the altar and publicly accepted Jesus Christ as his Savior. But the call was more than that; Artemas also realized that the call was for him to spread God's word, to help change lives himself through the power of God's love.

So Artemas waited until the church emptied, stayed after the other saved souls had gone home, stayed because he wanted Reverend Hamby to know that he wanted not only to be like Jesus but to be like Reverend Hamby himself. He wanted to preach, to take the word of the Lord to distant places and especially to the young. Thinking of his brothers, he confided to Reverend Hamby that he regretted he had not reached this decision earlier when they were all still home and he could have done them more good.

Reverend Hamby listened gently and with patience, for he had witnessed many saved souls in his years of preaching the gospel. Sometimes, he knew, it was the emotion of the moment that brought the lost sinner to the altar, and the temptation of Satan could take him back just as quickly as God had pulled him forward. Such was the never-ending job in which he had spent all his adult life.

But then sometimes, all too seldom it seemed, there would come one like this young man, whom he knew for certain the Lord had a hold on, and would never let go. So he agreed to meet with Artemas the next morning at the church to talk about what came next.

Artemas was waiting for him when he got there, as intense as he had been the night before, like a horse headed for the barn, the old mountain preacher thought. Artemas had told him he did not want to waste any time. His siblings were on their own, and his father was in good enough health to make it on his own. "I want to be like you," Artemas had told him several times the night before. "I want to get in that saddle like you and Francis Asbury and George Whitefield and Charles and John Wesley have done. I want to ride for the Lord and I want to see children, like my brothers, learn things and improve their lives." And then, to Reverend Hamby's surprise, he added, "I want to go to the mountains. I want to preach and start a school."

"Are you ready to preach?" Hamby asked. "Have you ever preached a sermon? How do you know you can do it?"

"God will give me the words and He'll give me the strength," Artemas replied. "I've been reading and studying the Bible for years."

Then, wanting to be completely truthful, he quickly corrected himself and amended his statement, "Well, for over a year, at least. Ask me about it if you want to."

"What do you think about the miracles of the Bible?" the mountain preacher asked, catching Artemas off guard.

"I think," Artemas began to stammer, "I think miracles are made by God. They are not manmade." His mind was racing. He thought of the Old Testament miracles: "Like the Plagues—the frogs, the hailstorm, the boils and blains, and the Red Sea and the burning bush, all those miracles of Moses and Joshua." And then he thought of those of Jesus and started listing as many as he could: "Feeding the 5,000, calming the storm, walking on water, having the disciples put down their nets and catching all those fish . . . ." Artemas realized he sounded like a child reciting something at Sunday school, but he had not anticipated such a question and the preacher was not interrupting him. "And, of course, the two greatest: His virgin birth and His resurrection from the dead." Artemas was pleading for his answers to be adequate.

"You have studied the Holy Word, my son," Reverend Hamby said gently, "but how do they relate to the work you want to do? And why do you want to go to the mountains to do it? That's hard country and good but hard people. It won't be easy."

"I want to be like you," Artemas said once again. "I've heard you preach every night this week. I wanted to come forward that first night, but I wanted to hear more. I just wanted to keep hearing you."

"Don't say you want to be like me," Hamby admonished him. "Say you want to be like Jesus; that's who I want to be like." After a pause, he continued, "I'll go by and tell Presiding Elder Thomas about you on my way home if he's in Dahlonega. If he agrees he'll contact the Bishop and get his approval. He'll like the idea of a school. He's big on education. That might sell him. And someday I want you to see what Bud Miller is doing with his school in Choestoe. He's a strong Methodist and a born teacher. You'll be impressed." He paused, then added, "And surprised. You'll be hearing from someone with more authority than me. Keep your powder dry and pray this is God's desire."

When Artemas got home that night, once again he could not sleep. In his twenty-six years on earth, Artemas had hardly been out of Upson and Monroe counties. He had, of course, seen the local wonders: the Great Swamp, Minona Springs, which the Creek Indians believed had healing waters; he had crossed the Flint River on the Wannamaker Ferry and marveled at the Montezuma Bluffs where fifty million years ago that part of Georgia was seabed. But he had never seen a mountain, not even Stone Mountain up there around Atlanta, much less the Appalachians that were said to be the oldest mountains in the world.

He continued to replay his awkward answer to Reverend Hamby's question about miracles and vowed to himself that he would do more study on that important part of the Bible. He wished he had had the forethought to mention Saul's conversion. That was a miracle of the highest order. Here was a tent maker who persecuted Christians and consented to the stoning of Stephen, and then on that road to Damascus, the sudden blaze of heavenly light shone around him "as the brightness of the sun." And then he heard that majestic voice of Jesus asking, "Saul, Saul, why persecutest thou me?" He was blinded and would be for three days and nights and then, Artemas remembered, "scales fell from his eyes."

Then there was that total surrender of self that transformed the vicious persecutor into the "very chiefest of the apostles." It was one of the great miracles in the Bible, one of Artemas's favorite stories, and he had been so nervous from the preacher's question he had completely forgotten it. He felt so dumb.

Or Peter's deliverance from prison where he was chained to two soldiers—one on either wrist—and constantly guarded before he was to be executed as James had been. There was no hope of escape, but the other disciples knew of God's miraculous powers, so they prayed "without ceasing." They knew what prayer could do. So did Peter, who calmly slept. Then the angel smote him, the big iron gates of the prison opened on their own accord, and Peter was delivered out of the dungeon.

"Why didn't I think of that miracle?" Artemas continued to beat himself up until finally, close to daybreak, he, like Peter, began to sleep. Perhaps an angel would be with him, he dreamed.

Telling his father the next morning of his plans turned out to be easier than Artemas had thought. The older Lester had watched his son the past year inch closer and closer to surrendering himself completely to the Lord. He was not surprised at that. What surprised him was that Artemas wanted to go into the mountain wilderness; he had thought his son's work would be closer to home, preaching over at The Rock or Musella, for example. But he never mentioned that.

The father remembered that March day in 1857 when Artemas was born on the farm on Echeconee Creek not far from Culloden. The Lesters were Scotch-Irish, only three generations removed from Britain with a one-generation stopover in Elbert County. He thought of his son's mother, Flora McDonald, and the shock of losing her in 1871. He was proud of the way Artemas, who was only a teenager at the time, had stepped in and helped keep the family together. Artemas didn't get to go to college, but two of his brothers had attended college and became lawyers. "You've been a wonderful son. I don't know what we would have done without you when your maw died," the reticent father said to his reticent son. His born-again son.

CHAPTER 2

The Journey

Artemas heard from Presiding Elder A. C. Thomas, but it was not the answer he had expected. The church would be glad to have him as a new itinerant preacher. His credentials looked sufficient, and, of course, the Reverend Hamby's strong and spirited endorsement had helped his case. But the church wanted him to get a year's experience before accepting the challenge to circuit ride in the mountains. So in 1884, Artemas spent a year—"a year of preparation," as Elder Thomas described it—in Lincolnton, Lincoln County, Georgia, near Augusta on the South Carolina line. It was cotton and tobacco country, and it was named not for Abraham but for Benjamin Lincoln, the Revolutionary War general. It had been created in 1796 just a few years after the Constitution was ratified and there was a United States. "Your grandfather once lived in that area," Mr. Lester said in an effort to encourage his son. "That's the Broad River Valley of Georgia. Petersburg is right there were the Broad runs into the Savannah. Bishop Francis Asbury spent a lot of time in that area spreading Methodism. And so did John Andrew; he was a Puritan who came there, ran a store, preached a little, and did some school teaching. He had a son named James who was a great Methodist bishop before the big war. He owned slaves, and that's what started the controversy that split the Methodist Church into the Southern and Northern divisions. Yep, it was Andrews who did that."

Artemas was both surprised and impressed that his father knew and remembered that history. "Lot of old Virginians were in that area," Mr. Lester continued. "Called 'em 'Goose Pond Virginians,' I reckon because they lived in that area where the ducks and geese migrating would stop and rest a while on a pond made by the flood-waters of the rivers. Best I remember, they broke up that big Wilkes

County area into at least four counties, Elbert, Oglethorpe, Wilkes, and Lincoln. Bunch of Georgia governors came out of there. Lot of duels fought in the early days, hot heads, a lot of them were."

The year passed slowly, providing Artemas ample opportunity to question not only his purpose for being in Lincoln County but for joining the ministry itself. "A testing time," Reverend Hamby had called it in one of the two letters Artemas received from him that year. "I don't see how he had time to write these," he mentioned to Mr. Lewis, the song leader in the church, who had befriended him.

During much of his time in Lincolnton, Artemas stayed with the Ross and Norman families, who took him in and made him feel welcome. Artemas knew he did not make friends easily, and that sometimes bothered him. Not enough, however, to change his ways, for Artemas was one of those souls who could live within himself. He would always be that way, single minded, not caring much about the impression he made and not given to regret, remorse, recrimination, or looking back. In late November he left Lincoln County and never returned. That would be his style and manner for the rest of his life.

After only a couple of weeks home, including Christmas, he was anxious to move on to his next assignment. He was pleased to find his father in good health and learn that another brother had become a lawyer. He got a ride with this brother in his new buggy back to Barnesville, where the brother had set up practice. There Artemas caught a train to Atlanta, and after waiting overnight he was able to get a hack to Dahlonega.

Before he got there, the terrain began to change, small hills became larger hills, and they became mountains. The driver kept the mules at a lope, and Artemas wondered what the hurry was. The mules would wheeze and snort, and their misty breath seemed to freeze in the winter air. Dahlonega was the site of the first big gold rush in the United States. Artemas realized he knew little, almost next to nothing, about it and vowed somehow to study that period of half a century before. Also, he realized, the same was true about the removal of the Indians in the mountains where he was going. He could have kicked himself for not concentrating on this local history and geography before now.

He knew they had had the nation's first gold rush, but he wasn't sure of the dates. And he knew that the Cherokees had been removed, but again he couldn't remember the details. All he knew was that it had been long before he was born.

Presiding Elder A. C. Thomas welcomed Artemas as soon as he arrived in town, evidently knowing almost the exact time the hack would arrive. There under a gigantic oak tree on the southeast corner of the Dahlonega square, the two Methodist ministers finally met. Thomas took Artemas nearby to his home, where Mrs. Thomas fed him a good meal of hog jowl with dried blackeyed peas and made him feel at home. Thomas was a talkative man, which suited Artemas just fine since he always found it a little difficult to carry on much of a conversation with a stranger.

Over supper, the Elder told Artemas that he wanted him to stay a week getting to know the local church folk and allow Thomas to give him a short course on mountain ways. It was what Artemas had wanted. He needed a history lesson, and Elder Thomas wasted no time in giving him one that first night.

"Most of the mountain people are Scotch-Irish like you. Their ancestors came here in five great waves beginning around 1717. They first came to Quaker William Penn's welcoming colony of Pennsylvania because of its religious tolerance and democratic ideals. They then came southward by Conestoga wagon, packhorses, and even on foot with all they could carry on their backs. Their main route was to the southwest through Virginia's Shenandoah Valley and down the Great Blue Ridge by way of the Indian's Old Warriors Trail, which some called the Great Philadelphia Wagon Road. They poured into the mountain wilds of North and South Carolina, Eastern Tennessee, and Northern Georgia. Some others crossed the Cumberland Gap into Kentucky.

"Artemas, I'm telling you about one of the greatest movements of people in American history, some 400,000 before 1776. Scotch-Irish were hop-scotching over fellow Scotch-Irish in search of the dreamed-of spots where they could shake off the tyrannies of their past and be truly free men on their own terms. Those colonists on the coast and Piedmont were thankful and relieved to have these fierce individuals as buffers against the Indians who were becoming more and more hostile.

"Most of the Scotch-Irish brought along their small pot-stills, which they transported slung under their ark-like wagons, tied to their packhorses, or even strapped onto their own backs. Nearly all of them had learned how to build a whiskey still rig from the Germans of Pennsylvania, from whom they also obtained their deadly accurate long squirrel rifles.

"Mountain people learned early on that their survival mainly was dependent upon their finding and producing their own food. There were no centers of commerce, and only a few stores were available that carried rudimentary staples like salt, flour, lard, sugar, and coffee. Necessity forced them into an existence of 'Make Do or Do Without.' You ever heard that?

"Food production was made difficult by the mountain terrain. Of course, there were the rich, fertile valleys, but they were far too few. Many were limited to what produce they could scratch out of the rocky hillsides and what their animals could forage for themselves in the thickets and on the mountain balds. That pretty well limited then to corn as their staple crop and razorback hogs as their principal meat animals. It is no wonder then that the diet of Appalachia came to be known as 'Old Cornbread and Sowbelly.'

"Some of the farms were almost perpendicular, often tilled to a 45-degree angle where the corn had to be hoed on one's knees and often propped up with rocks to keep it from falling downhill. Plowing was done with a steer pulling a 'bull tongue,' which was a sharpened stick with a metal rim. Rows were curved to the contour of the land and also to miss the boulders and dead trunks of trees killed by girdling and left to stand until they rotted and fell. Plantings were mainly of corn with some rye and a little oats raised along the creeks, and after planting all cultivation of the corn was by hoe, usually by the women and children of the household. It was a hard life. Still is, my boy! That's enough for tonight; let's go to bed."

Over breakfast the next morning, the Elder continued his lesson. "This place is kinda dead in the winter, but come summer you can't stir the people in town with a stick; 'course, years ago it was a mob scene with all the miners and speculators." From his enthusiasm, it was obvious that the Elder would like to have lived during that exciting time. "Camp meetings are still big, and it's not just the Baptists. There's Amicalola in Dawson, Yellow Creek in Hall, and Mossy Creek and Loudsville just over in White. They say Loudsville in the '30s was filled with folks from all over—mostly Buncomb County, North Carolina, just waiting to pile into Cherokee territory when they opened it up. You'll be going through there; that's on your way to your new assignment."

Elder Thomas had already found him a mule. "You'll need a gentle one," he said, almost as if he were talking to a child. "And we'll get up the provisions later. But I want you to stay around here a few days and get a feel for this place and these mountain people. I didn't mention Cedar Camp Ground, that may be the oldest 'round here. Some call it 'Woolhat Campground.' That's what a lot of these oldtimers wear, you know.

"The services at Cedar were usually held in October, need a fire then. You ought to see it at night with all the pine knots blazing. They have four services a day, at eight in the morning, then eleven o'clock, then three in the afternoon, and one at night. Eleven o'clock on Sunday, that's the main one. 'Round here it's saved for Uncle Newt Austin. You talk about raining down the cannonballs on the sinners, there's no escape when he's preaching. Uncle Tate Seabolt and Uncle Cader Stancil, they weren't preachers, but you could hardly have a camp meeting without them; they were big-hearted men. There's a lot of talking about moving ole Cedar in closer to Dahlonega, but that hasn't happened yet. By the way, there's a Negro campground about three miles from here called 'Lizard Lope,' and they have good services with both black and white attending. Most all our churches have special balconies; the war's over isn't it? We're all God's children."

Artemas continued to nod, and Elder Thomas continued to talk. "I want you to see a couple of our schools. I know that's what you're interested in. We've got over thirty school houses in this county and I want to call one 'Liddia.' You know who that was?" Before Artemas could answer, Thomas told him, "Paul's first convert at Macedonia. We just did something I think is going to work well—a board of trustees in each militia district to oversee the school. Here in Dahlonega it's A. G. Wimpy and Allen Gaddis. They run everything around here and Jane McDaniel. In Auraria it's Joe T. Miller, and I forgot who else. Jonas Seabolt in Chestatee, Moses Waters in Nimblewill; it's organized to a fare thee well. They've also have set up the County Institute, which will be a weekly meeting of the teachers, and they'll have an expert there to talk with them and bring them up to date. Has to be a college graduate."

Artemas noticed how he said that, as if college graduates knew everything about everything, and he couldn't help shrinking a little because he wasn't one. But he did have one piece of information Elder Thomas did not know or probably had forgotten. While they were eating one night, the Elder asked, "Where did the name 'Artemas' come from? Is it a family name?"

"It's in the Bible," a surprised Artemas answered.

The Elder was flabbergasted. "Where?" he sputtered.

Artemas delighted in enlightening him. "Paul, in his letter to Titus, chapter 3 verse 12." The Elder got up from the table, went over to his desk and picked up the Bible, turned to Titus, read quickly, and looked up. "So it is. I remember now, he was to replace Titus in Crete and Titus was then to rejoin Paul in Necopalis."

The next day, the Elder took Artemas to visit Lewis School at the Frogtown law ground. They left before daylight and didn't return until after dark. In the days following, Artemas got a good feeling for the community and Elder Thomas. He met Reverend T. G. Christian, another Methodist preacher, and learned that Reverend Milfred Hamby was also his mentor and had pastored his church as a young man in the 1850s right before the war. He also met Dr. H. C. Whelchel, who was thinking about moving his medical practice from Gainesville to Dahlonega. And he talked with the oldest merchant in the town, A. G. Wimpy, who told of a young Joe Brown coming to town from the Canada District in nearby Union County "with pails of butter in a sack and a string of chickens thrown over the horse and several baskets of eggs. We'd pay Joe for them; he'd get what the family needed and head back home." Artemas loved the next descriptive sentence of that young man who would dominate Georgia politics for half a century: "Joe wasn't one to tarry or idle around."

At this time, there was still talk in Dahlonega that Frank and Jesse James had come through the county a few years before in 1881 on their way to Lula, Georgia, after robbing an army paymaster in Muscle Shoals, Alabama. Their great-grandfather, William James, had fought in the Revolutionary War near Augusta and then lived in Petersburg after the war. His children and grandchildren later migrated to Logan County, Kentucky, where Frank was born, and then into Missouri where Jesse was born. The brothers then went on to become the best-known outlaws in the country after the Civil War. But they kept many of their Georgia ties. In 1882, Jesse was murdered, and Frank was captured and brought to Alabama in 1884 for trial. He was found "not guilty" even though seven of twenty witnesses positively identified him. So the county was still buzzing over the famous brother outlaws being in their area just a few years earlier.

The Presiding Elder never mentioned that Artemas was not college educated, and Artemas never brought up the fact that he had been surprised how easy it had been for him to become an itinerant preacher. He could only conclude that his desire and his character had been enough to persuade Reverend Hamby, and that good man's reputation and word had been enough for the Presiding Elder.

Of course, the salary was very low; Artemas would make about fifty cents a day for the year ahead, if that. But what was it Bishop Francis Asbury had once said? "Our poverty is our purity." The man he said it to noted that, at the time, Asbury "had a large rent in his coat at the back of his shoulder."

There was a shortage of Methodist itinerants in the last quarter of the nineteenth century. But there was no shortage of "organization." At the time there was the Methodist Episcopal Church, the Methodist Protestant Church, and the Methodist Episcopal Church South. In 1876, the Methodist Episcopal Church had divided along racial lines, and the white membership was reduced to 2,677 in 1880.

The itinerants had to be men of great faith, willing to endure many hardships. Some called them "riders of the long road." One description was that they were men "of defiant energy, unyielding zeal, and matchless courage, who laughed at hardships, welcomed perils, and triumphed over indescribable difficulties." While not educated as much as others in the ministry, some were even illiterate themselves. They were subject, however, to the same rigorous regulations set up by the General Conference, which insisted the intellectual was secondary to the spiritual. It was emphasized, "You have nothing to do but to save souls . . . to bring as many sinners as you possibly can to repentance." They were also expected to have short hair, be clean shaven, and wear a broad-brimmed hat. Such was the life young Artemas Lester had chosen for himself.

CHAPTER 3

History 'Round a Stove

"Before I leave here," Artemas had told the Elder several times, "I want to learn more about the gold rush. It would be a shame to have come through here and not know much of anything about it, don't you think?"

So one cold Saturday morning Reverend Thomas took his young South Georgia friend down to Wimpy's store to see if some local "ole timers" might be hanging around the potbellied stove on a cold winter morning and be willing to spin a few tales. They were in luck; there were several who had been young men when the excitement had taken place those many years before. Artemas recognized among them the names Ravan, Cavendar, Grizzle, Rider, Stancil, and Lance. All were ready and eager to take a trip down memory lane. Artemas told them he remembered his father saying, "Thar's gold in them thar hills." Mr. Lester believed, as did most, that this cry of gold-fevered prospectors originated in the California Gold Rush of 1849. But that was a myth, the Lumpkin County oldtimers told Artemas, and he quickly found out that it came from the colorful prose of Mark Twain's *The Guilded Age*.

With some pride, Mr. Cavendar said the saying came straight out of Dahlonega, Georgia. "It was the plea of Dr. Matthew F. Stephenson. He was the assayer of the United States Branch Mint that was located here. You see, he wanted the miners to stay here rather than being tempted by what they might find in California."

Mr. Rider interrupted, saying Dr. Stephenson was convinced that Georgia was one of the richest mineral states in the nation, and so one day he got out on the balcony of the Lumpkin County Courthouse in Dahlonega and pointed in the direction of Findley Ridge half a mile to the south and yelled. "Why go to California? In that ridge lies more gold than man ever dreamt of. There's millions in it!"

"And the good doctor knew what he was talking about." Mr. Grizzle spit a stream of tobacco juice and continued, "In less than a decade, Findley Ridge became the site of the richest gold strike in Georgia, known as 'The Findley Chute.' But many of the miners did not heed Stephenson's advice, and they went out to California and made that expression 'There's millions in it!' their rallying cry whenever they had a setback. Whenever a claim seemed barren or the prospector began talking about giving up, the Georgians would answer 'There's millions in it' and 'just keep on digging.'"

Reverend Thomas then interrupted. "Twain was collecting stories of the California gold fields when he heard it and attributed it to a character in his book, Colonel Mulberry Sellers. That gave it worldwide fame. Then over the years the words, 'There's millions in it!' became that more colorful mountain version your Daddy heard, 'There's gold in them thar hills!'"

"I'll tell you something else," Mr. Rider said, interrupting his interrupter. "Twain also missed the story of Georgia's 'Russell Boys'—William, Levi and Oliver—who left Lumpkin County in 1858 to prospect the eastern slopes of the Rockies and touched off the century's third major gold rush with their strike at Cherry Creek right in the shadow of Pike's Peak in Colorado. They founded a town there that they named after Georgia's Auraria. Later that settlement combined with and took the name of the one on the other side of the stream called 'Denver.' How about that for a little history, son?" He smiled, looking at an open-mouthed Artemas.

He wasn't finished. "And I'll tell you another thing: Twain did not mention another Georgia prospector, John Hamilton Gregory, who discovered near the Russells' diggings what came to be known as the Gregory Lode. It was the greatest single gold strike in America and was called 'the richest square mile on earth.'"

It was obvious that Mr. Rider had made a career of correcting history's failure to give credit to the impact the discovery and mining of gold in Dahlonega had on the growth and development of Southern Appalachia and the achievements of its people.

As Artemas continued to listen, he learned gold was discovered and mined in commercial quantities over a wide area of the eastern slopes of the Great Blue Ridge extending from western Maryland through northeastern Alabama and that four major belts were discovered in Georgia. The Dahlonega Belt was the richest and extended about 150 miles in length to varying widths of 2 to 6 miles. Mr. Cavendar had been that exact. The other three were the Hall County Belt, the Carroll County Belt, and the McDuffie County Belt, which some claimed to be the real site of the first discovery of gold in Georgia in 1823.

Mr. Wimpy wandered over when there were no customers and added with authority, "The when, where, and who of the first discovery of gold in Georgia will never be exactly known. The Cherokees knew about gold in and around Dahlonega from the time deSoto came looking for it. They called the bright yellow metal 'dalonigei.' They never placed the value on gold that the white men did, or maybe they just kept quiet about it because they knew all the turmoil it would cause."

Mr. Stancil said there had always been an argument over exactly what touched off the Great Georgia Gold Rush in the late 1820s. He explained there were at least three conflicting stories. "Now, Aunt Biddie will try to tell you that the sale of a gold nugget by an Indian boy living on Ward Creek to a white man named Jesse Hogan was how it happened. The Parks Family will tell you it was the kicking up of a gold-bearing quartz rock by fourteen-year-old Benjamin Parks while hunting deer, and then others will tell you it was the discovery of a three-ounce gold nugget by John Witherow on Duke's Creek at the site of what was to become the Nacoochee Mine in what was then Habersham but later became White County."

Again, Elder Thomas insisted on getting in on the history. "The Parks claim received more attention because he sold his mining lease to former vice president and United States senator John C. Calhoun of South Carolina and his son-in law, Thomas C. Clemson, who was a mining engineer."

"Yes," Wimpy interrupted, "using slave labor, Clemson and Calhoun made a mint of money! No one knows how much, but the mine was one of Georgia's richest, and Clemson later used much of his part of the fortune to found and endow Clemson University."

Two other old mountaineers had come in, and now one injected himself into the storytelling. "It was Calhoun who, with the help of Missouri senator Thomas Hart Benton, known as 'Old Bullion,' got the appropriation through Congress that established a branch mint in Dahlonega in 1837. It burned just a couple of years ago. They hauled the machinery for it all the way from Savannah, and it operated until it was seized by the state of Georgia at the beginning of the Civil War. It had recorded receipts of over six million dollars."

Mr. Cavendar corrected him. "But that figure was a fraction of the total amount because much of the gold was coined through private mints like that one established by Templeton Reid in Gainesville or shipped out by the Bank of Darien which had branches back then in Auraria and in Dahlonega."

Another mountaineer added, "The Dahlonega mint struck five-dollar gold coins known as 'Half Eagles' that had a 'D' on them. I've seen one. But during the Civil War the mint's machinery rusted and ruined and the building was later used as a school for the black children of the community."

Again Elder Thomas interjected, "In 1873, Congress donated the structure and site to the state of Georgia for educational purposes, and it became what is now North Georgia College, one of the nation's first military land grant colleges and coeducational from its beginning."

"Let me tell you about Auraria," Mr. Wimpy said. "It was the first county seat of Lumpkin County, and it had its boom and bust. Some will tell you that it was a wide-open mining town, like some of them places out west. But that's not right. It got that reputation because of William Gilmore Simms and that blasted book of his: *Guy Rivers: A Tale of Georgia.*

"Auraria was a law-abiding town. Even Simms, who visited the area for the first time fifteen years after he wrote his book, had to admit that he did not see a drunk, to say nothing of a rooster fight or gander pulling. Nevertheless, that make-believe character he created, Guy Rivers, continued to have a life of his own as a cunning criminal who terrorized gold diggers from a hideout in a wild cave on a cliff overlooking the Chestatee River."

Elder Thomas again picked up the story, and Artemas realized that this was not the first time the Thomas-Wimpy history lesson had been given to an audience. "Auraria had its beginning in the summer of 1832 when a squatter, William Dean—some of his relatives are over there where you are going—built a cabin on the ridge separating the westward-flowing Etowah and the southward-flowing Chestatee rivers by only two miles. It was a natural congregating point for the swarms of prospectors who invaded the waters of those two rivers and their tributary streams with their pans, spades, and rocker cradles. Dean was followed by a businessman, Nathaniel Nuckolls, who set up a small tavern, which catered to the thirst of miners for the strong ale. It was first called Dean's and later Nuckollsville, spelled with an 'N' not a 'K,' but they called it 'Knucklesville' with a 'K' because of the tendency of drunken miners to settle their disputes with their knuckles.

"Within the year there came to the community three leaders who gave it its name and character. The first was Mrs. George W. Paschal or 'Grandma Paschal' as she was called—the widow of a Revolutionary War soldier from Oglethorpe County. She brought her family with her, bought out the Nuckolls establishment, and set up a tavern in which no alcoholic beverages were served. She was a moral and religious woman and established a Baptist church there. She became known as the 'Angel of Auraria' for work with the sick and needy.

"The second was John C. Calhoun who established his mine on the claim he purchased from Benny Parks and who was determined to see that Auraria became a proper dignified community worthy of the presence of a politician like himself. He set about to find a better name than 'Knucklesville' and endorsed adoption of the one proposed by his South Carolina colleague, a Doctor Croft, who advocated the town be named Aureolo, meaning 'golden' or 'shining like gold,' and the county Aldoraddo, which he said was Spanish for 'gold region.'

"But it was a man named Major John Powell who came up with the name Auraria, which he said was Latin for 'gold mine.' The Georgia General Assembly named the county for Governor Wilson Lumpkin in recognition of his role as the prime mover in ridding the area of the Cherokees and establishing the ownership of their lands by lottery. The name Auraria stuck, although the official designation of the settlement was Lumpkin Court House until the county seat of Dahlonega six miles away was established in October 1833."

Three old-timers who had heard the story many times by now had left, but Mr. Cavendar hung in there. "By 1834 Auraria had a population of 1,000 people, although some estimates put it as high as 4,000 and that of the county at 10,000, It was a settlement of 100 dwelling houses, 20 stores, 5 taverns, 3 physicians, 3 tailors, a branch of the Bank of Darien, a newspaper called *The Western Messenger*, and more than 200 gold mines. It also had 15 lawyers, because of the preoccupation of everyone with land titles and the litigation that resulted from them."

"Yeah," a man called Uncle Archie interrupted. "This was good because disputes that were settled with guns in the streets out west wound up in court in Georgia, and only one murder was recorded in the entire history of Auraria."

The history lesson continued as Artemas sat entranced. One reason assigned for the choice of Dahlonega over Auraria as the county seat of Lumpkin County, it seemed, was the number of disputed land titles growing out of the fact that the lot on which Auraria was situated had been drawn in the Georgia lottery by a family of orphans living in Newton County. As one might expect, there were a number of lawsuits over clouded land titles.

Uncle Archie seemed to know more about this than the others. "With all this litigation, uncertainty about Auraria's future, the flimsy construction of its buildings, and its failure to become the county seat all began the decline for Auraria. And then the California Gold Rush of 1849 sealed it. Many miners left for the West, business and governmental affairs picked up in Dahlonega, and all this reduced the population of Auraria to less than 300. When Grandma Paschal's son George returned from Texas for a visit in 1858, he said the town had decayed and disappeared. Grandma Paschal continued to live there and, after her death in 1869, was buried in the Auraria Baptist Cemetery beside her husband, whose body she had moved there at the height of Auraria's boom."

For the first time, Artemas had a question. "Where did the name 'Dahlonega' come from?"

Elder Thomas beat Uncle Archie to the answer. "It's derived from the Cherokee word for gold. It went through a series of spellings. One was 'Talonaga' with a 'T.' Finally its pronunciation and spelling were straightened out by a Cherokee Indian who said it correctly should be with a 'D' so it became Dahlonega.

"It started as a small clearing where Benny Parks and Lewis Ralston had a 'licklog' to salt their stock, and then later it was a campsite for hundreds of miners. When it was chosen as the county seat by the five justices of the governing Inferior Court of Lumpkin County, its first permanent building was a log cabin built to house the sessions of the Superior Court. The first contractor to build a permanent courthouse defaulted in 1834, and the second one completed the project in 1836. It is said that he put a Bible under each of the four cornerstones and built it of bricks made from local clay."

Mr. Rider joined in again. "This town is sitting on top of a rich gold vein; we're the only city this side of heaven that literally may have 'streets of gold.' Just recently they were digging on the city's main streets and uncovered a vein of gold two feet thick and very rich. The city council removed several pounds of ore, and I hear they are going to display it at one of them expositions in Atlanta."

Mr. Cavendar clarified, "The first mining in Lumpkin, White, Habersham, Hall and all these surrounding counties was done by individuals digging up and washing out the sand and gravel of the banks and beds of streams and the sides of the hills."

When Artemas came through, he could still see how the digging had transformed the land in many places into a pitted landscape and that the courses of many of the branches and tributaries of the Etowah and Chestatee rivers had been altered by the diggings. "Looks like it would have been wasteful," he said.

"Yes," Cavendar answered. "Even those who could afford to use some of the expensive washing machines peddled back then only captured about half of the gold present in the dirt and rock they handled. The typical miner, using a shovel, pan, and rocker cradle, was lucky to average five to ten pennyweights of gold a day, unless he had the good fortune of finding a big nugget or discovering a rich vein.

"Some firms developed a pioneering technique of hydraulic mining, which was written up in all the mining textbooks as the 'Dahlonega Method.' It involved the displacement of gold from the side and tops of the mountains through the power of water sprayed through pressurized pipes the same way that fire hoses put out fires in tall buildings. Miles of pipe were laid into the mountains; the longest stretch was 29 miles. And countless streams of water were sprayed upon the mountaintops, washing the gold-bearing rocks, gravel, and dirt into the valleys below. There they were crushed in huge stamping mills and washed over mercury-coated plates, which attracted and held the gold. The vibrations from the stamping mills in full operation were said to literally shake the mountains like earthquakes."

"And don't forget," Mr. Grizzle interjected, "the operation of history's first diving bell from a boat on the Chestatee River. But there is no record of how much gold they got from the beds of sand in that way."

"Yes," Mr. Rider added. "Hard facts on the production and income from individual mines will never be known. Calhoun never revealed any figures about the fortune he earned. Of the documented fortunes made in Dahlonega gold, the greatest was that realized by Samuel J. Tilden, the man who lost the presidency to Rutherford B. Hayes in 1876 by one vote in the electoral college. He bought the holdings of former president Ulysses S. Grant and others for $500,000 and proceeded to make more than $4,000,000 from the tons of ore he washed out of his claims with water carried through a ditch 30 miles long he had dug for the operations."

It had been the history lesson Artemas had wanted. He thanked them for educating him, and he and the Elder continued their conversation over a wonderful supper Mrs. Thomas had waiting. Before they went to bed for the night, Reverend Thomas promised a similar lesson from Miss Biddie Davis, the elderly Cherokee woman who had lived through another part of mountain history that he thought Artemas needed to hear.

Miss Biddie Remembers

The small, elderly, no-nonsense Cherokee woman was ready and waiting when Artemas and Elder Thomas arrived at her neat little home about two miles from the square. Miss Biddie Davis was telling her story before they had even sat down.

"I know you will think it's just me talking, but the Cherokees were different and special. They knew they were a breed apart and proudly called themselves the 'Ani Yunwiya,' which means 'the principal people.' Their attributes were recognized by the first white men who came in contact with them beginning with Hernando deSoto in 1540." Adjusting herself, she leaned forward. "And later, Father Roget, a Jesuit missionary who visited the Southern Indians with Spanish explorers in the 1560s, wrote that the Cherokees were 'superior' to any Indians he encountered.

"Read this," she said as she handed Artemas a faded clipping. It was by a man named Henry Timberlake, an early explorer who described the Cherokees as "handsome and proud." He said they had an advanced culture that put them several notches above all other aboriginal Americans with the possible exception of the Mayan and Aztec groups. But even that conclusion, Artemas read aloud, must be tempered by "the fact of history that the Cherokees obviously possessed a capacity to adapt, evolve, and survive while their Mayan and Aztec counterparts did not."

Miss Biddie expounded, "You see, those others built pyramids, prized riches, made human sacrifices, resisted their invaders, and perished. The Cherokees built towns, established a government and a newspaper, believed in a Supreme Being, welcomed visitors, and learned from them.

"That's the kind of people we were," she said after giving Artemas time to read one of the many articles she had saved for years. "But no people ever pay a dearer price for their achievement and promise than we did.

"There were probably 25,000 Cherokees living in these mountains when deSoto came west of here. They lived in about 200 villages in a territory from the Ohio River on the north to the Tennessee River on the south and the Savannah River on the east. They were divided into seven clans or families following the blood lines of the mothers known as Wolf, Deer, Bird, Red Paint, Wild Potato, Long Hair and Twister.

"Each village had two chiefs—a white or peace chief who directed domestic affairs concerning everything from spring planting to fall harvest and a red or war chief who commanded during winter, which was a time of war. Each village also had a seven-sided town house (one side for each clan) in which all residents met to decide community matters on a democratic, one-person/one-vote basis without regard to sex. In addition, each had its special group of leading females known as War Women or Pretty Women who wielded great influence in the determination of war strategy and made binding decisions on the fate of captives."

She quickly continued, "Women were the leaders in village life, and, except for hunting, we had an equal voice in all matters. We played the dominant roles in clan regulations and the upbringing of the children. Cherokees traced their lineage through the female, and it was the male who moved to the home and clan of the bride after marriage.

"Each village was self-sustaining within the confederation of four districts—Overhill, Lower, Middle, and Valley. Within each district, one of the strongest villages was informally recognized as the capital, and during times of strife that is where their chiefs met to plan courses of action for the tribe. Other American Indian tribes moved around a lot and lived in portable teepees; Cherokees established permanent, fenced villages of log and clay dwellings.

"When the missionaries came, the Cherokees insisted that they set up schools for their children. There was a Moravian mission at Spring Place over in Murray County not far from here. Sometimes the brightest students would be sent to Cornwall, Connecticut, to continue their education."

Obviously, Miss Biddie had told this story many times. "They planted, tended, and harvested crops in communal fields and were skilled in the art of cultivation. Our produce was supplemented through fishing and hunting. The Cherokees had never seen horses before deSoto brought them, and sometimes they would eat horse-meat, but never dogs or cats. One of the old beliefs was that raw fish would cure the whooping cough and that eating a live fish would make one a better swimmer.

"The women tended the crops while the men hunted, fished, repaired homes and fences, dug out canoes, and made blowguns and bows and arrows. Our year was organized around six major festivals—the First New Moon of Spring, the New Green Corn, the Green Corn, the October New Moon, the Establishment of Friendship and Brotherhood, and the Bouncing Bush. There last two were designed for purification from past sins and hardships and cleansing of the village, our homes, and ourselves for the new year. It was at this time that we allowed the return and rehabilitation of past offenders who had escaped punishment by making their way to villages of refuge. Every seventh year we had a seventh festival, the Uku Dance, marking the inauguration of the principal white chief.

"We had legends passed down through generations. Many thought that bears were men who had wandered off to live in the forest and had a saying, 'Don't be too friendly with the bears, you may become one.' Our ancestors believed that the mountains were made by a great buzzard that pulled up the earth with its claws. And that Walasiyi was a giant frog that hopped from mountaintop to mountaintop not far from here. They believed in small fairies, the yun-wee-chuns-dee, who lived in caves and looked after children and those lost in the mountains." She paused, looking at her two preacher guests. "And we also believed in evil spirits.

"Cherokees loved athletics and had an organized system of competition among the clans and villages in the game of 'anetsa' or 'stick ball.'"

"Like lacrosse," Elder Thomas interjected and then continued, "it was a rough-and-tumble game in which opposing teams sought to move a ball made of stuffed animal skin from the center of a measured field across the goal lines at either end, using small wooden sticks with netted ends for scooping, carrying, or throwing the ball. The ball could not be touched with the hands, and the levels of violent contact often resulted in severe injuries and even death. The first team to score 20 points won. Sometimes they would wager land on the outcome of the game. Ball Ground in Cherokee County, Georgia, got its name because one tribe beat another in a fierce, three-day ball game there in 1818 with 1,000 acres being the bet."

Miss Biddie gave the Elder a look that seemed to say, "Who's telling this story?" But the Elder would not be deterred. He continued, "The Cherokees' belief system paralleled Christianity in many respects, and this made it easy for them to be converted. They believed in a Great One, Uhalotega, or 'he who sitteth above,' who created heaven above and earth below and who would punish or reward human spirits after death. They revered nature, freedom of the individual, and stressed cooperation over conflict."

Now Miss Biddie interrupted. "Yes, but the early settlers were also shocked at how Cherokees entered and ended the marital relationship with ease. Divorce was such a simple process that it could be achieved by the female just placing her husband's belongings outside the dwelling or by the male merely moving out of the wife's house."

Miss Biddie leaned forward as if she were about to say something important. "The man more responsible than any other for the development of the Cherokee people as the most civilized, cultured, and best-governed tribe of American Indians was not a chief, but a crippled, illiterate silversmith named George Guest. He was the half-breed son of an emissary sent to the Cherokee Nation by President George Washington. His Indian name was 'Sequoyah,' which meant 'possum in a poke.' He spent twenty years of his life developing a Cherokee alphabet of eighty-six characters that looked like a combination of English, Greek, and a bunch of other letters and characters—one for each sound in the Cherokee tongue."

Miss Biddie looked sad as she continued, "He was ridiculed, accused of witchcraft, had all his work thrown into the fireplace by his wife and his house burned by his enemies. They called his efforts 'pheasant tracks criss-crossing each other in light snow.' But things changed when he demonstrated before the National Council with his six-year-old daughter that any person who knew the Cherokee vocabulary and could memorize the alphabet could write and read. Finally, the council gave its blessing, and in 1821, when I was five years old, adopted what was called the Sequoyah Syllabary as the Cherokee national language. I learned it as a little child."

Again, the Elder picked up the story. "This began the greatest demonstration of mass education in history. Sequoyah trained an army of young tutors who held classes throughout the Cherokee Nation, and soon every child and adult was committing to memory his Cherokee characters. Students who had spent two years in missionary school without learning how to write basic English were producing fluent Cherokee. It really was the forerunner of universal education and the phonics approach to teaching reading."

Miss Biddie shifted in her chair. "Of course, then came a national newspaper known as *The Cherokee Phoenix*." Glancing again at her two-preacher audience, she said, "The first words to be printed in the Cherokee language were the first five verses of Genesis. A printing press was set up in New Echota, and Elias Boudinot was named the editor. The first issue of the paper came out in February 1828."

Again, Miss Biddie looked sad as she gazed into the fireplace and remembered. "Things would never be the same in the Cherokee Nation. The Cherokees would be removed within the decade, and Boudinot would be fired as editor in 1832 because he advocated acceptance of the removal. The paper continued under a new editor, John Ross's brother-in-law, Elijah Hicks, but it went bankrupt and was discontinued two years later."

Elder Thomas could not resist adding, "With its printing press, the Cherokee Council not only published its newspaper but also turned out a translation of the New Testament and prepared a spelling book and an official compilation of all the Cherokee laws. Think about it," he said with admiration. "They disseminated the printed word to a nearly 100 percent literate population. That has never been achieved by any other nation. Emissaries sent into the area often found the Cherokees were better informed about the issues than they were."

"Yes, it was great progress," Miss Biddie said, as she got up and prepared tea for her visitors, "but then came a 700-mile journey so cruel and miserable that it became known in history as 'The Trail of Tears.' It took the lives of one-quarter of the Cherokee Nation. The two Cherokee leaders at this time were Major Ridge, speaker of the National Council, and John Ross, president of the National Committee. It was Ridge who conspired with the Andrew Jackson administration to implement a final treaty of removal, and it was Ross who, after exhausting every resource of opposition, had the terrible task of leading his people to the new western nation.

"You see," Miss Biddie explained, "we had accepted at face value all we had been told by every American president from George Washington on: that if we would follow 'the white man's path' and assimilate ourselves into the culture of the white man, we would be cared for. Thomas Jefferson bragged on us for our establishing our own republican form of government. President James Monroe visited us; President John Quincy Adams approved our new National Constitution. We fought on the side of the United States in the War of 1812 under the command of General Andrew Jackson, and we thought he would continue to be our friend after his election as president in 1828."

Here she stopped; it seemed as if she could hardly go on. The Elder picked up. "They could not have been more mistaken because the Jackson administration's actions were their undoing. And a fact that is particularly ironic is that Cherokee chief Junaluska who saved Jackson's life in the Battle of Horseshoe Bend was rudely dismissed by Jackson when sent to Washington as an emissary of the Cherokees."

"My father knew the chief personally," Miss Biddie said, "and later when Junaluska was on the Trail of Tears, he witnessed the death of a Cherokee mother with one baby strapped to her back and leading two other children. It is said that Junaluska, with tears coursing down his cheeks, lifted his cap, turned his face to the sky, and cried, 'Oh, my God, if I had known at the Battle of Horseshoe Bend what I know now, American history would have been differently written.'" Miss Biddie then sank lower in her chair.

The Elder continued for her. "Many Cherokees—about 5,000—voluntarily had already gone west; Sequoyah was one of them. Remember, in 1828, two historic events occurred. Andrew Jackson was elected president, and gold was discovered in Cherokee territory. In less than a year, more than 10,000 gold-crazy prospectors poured into the eastern part of the Cherokee Nation. The Cherokee National Council ordered the intruders out, and federal troops were called in, but they didn't help. Then the Georgia General Assembly enacted a law extending the state's sovereignty over Cherokee territory in December 1829 and petitioned President Jackson to remove the federal troops, which he promptly did.

"The Georgia Legislature then ordered the Georgia Guard to control the area and prohibited the meeting of any Cherokee governmental body except to cede land. Two missionaries, including a Reverend Worcester, were arrested, tried, convicted, and imprisoned for being in the territory without licenses. The Cherokee Nation then hired themselves a Philadelphia lawyer named William Wirt and took the whole issue to the United States Supreme Court."

Miss Biddie had long ago memorized the details. "Congress barely passed a Removal Act in 1830, which provided for the exchange of eastern Cherokee lands for comparable amounts of territory in the west. President Jackson then appointed a superintendent of Cherokee removal."

"Now this is historic, Artemas," the Elder said, growing more serious. "With Chief Justice John Marshall presiding, the Supreme Court in February 1832 ruled in the case of *Worcester v. Georgia* that all of Georgia's Indian laws were null and void and only the United States Government could legislate for Indians. It ordered Worcester and Reverend Elizur Butler released and enjoined the state of Georgia from taking further actions against the Cherokees. And you know how President Jackson responded? He ignored it; he said, 'John Marshall has made his ruling; now let him enforce it.'

"Jackson said the decision was an effort to embarrass him in an election year and encouraged Governor Wilson Lumpkin to continue Georgia's activities. So Georgia created Cherokee County out of Indian lands and provided for the election of officials to govern it from among Georgians living in the territory. Missionaries were ordered out of the area and their property seized.

"Principal Chief John Ross opposed removal with every means at his disposal and was jailed on several occasions for his activities. President Jackson, realizing the matter never would be resolved in dealing with Ross, summoned him to Washington for consultations while at the same time sending a New York clergyman, Reverend John F. Schermerhorn, to Georgia to negotiate a secret treaty with a minority group of Cherokees composed of Major Ridge and nineteen others. It was called the Treaty of New Echota, and it was signed in December 1835 by Major Ridge, John Ridge, Elias Boudinot, and Stan Watie and ratified by a one-vote majority in the United States Senate and declared law by President Jackson in May 1836. It proposed a payment of $3,500,000 and a grant of 7 million acres in Indian Territory. Later, the amount was increased to $5,000,000. The treaty was rejected by the Cherokee National Council, and a petition gathered by Cherokee vice chief George Lowery contained 15,904 Cherokee signatures or almost 100 percent of the 16,000 Cherokees believed living in the eastern United States at that time."

The Elder continued, "The Jackson administration ignored it and gave the Cherokee Nation two years to remove its citizens west. When no voluntary efforts were made by the Cherokees to relocate themselves within the allotted period, President Martin Van Buren ordered General Winfield Scott and an army of 9,500 to forcibly remove them."

Miss Biddie reflected, "Scott was an interesting character who would go on to play an important role in the war with Mexico and twice would be nominated to run for president. He was known as 'Old Fuss and Feathers.' A tall, 6-foot-3, heavy man with bushy brows, he liked to cook and eat. He took pride in his ability to bake good bread, and he loved soup."

The Elder laughed. "Yes, that would be one reason he would be defeated in his political career because at that time soup was considered a very sissy dish. He was fifty years old, tactless, and overly strict. He was an Episcopalian who attended church often but was so big he could not kneel and would just sit through the service with his head bowed as if in prayer.

"He set up his headquarters called 'The Station' in Lumpkin County between Auraria and Dahlonega. You can still see the signs of where it was. His men built more than thirty stockades in the Cherokee territory, one, I think, in Brasstown Valley where you're going, at a placed called Mineral Springs, and another near Morganton called Fort Chastain."

Once more Miss Biddie reached into a drawer filled with old yellowed papers that she had set on the floor for this lesson. She handed Artemas a copy of Scott's orders to his soldiers dated May 17, 1838:

> Every possible kindness, compatible with necessity of removal, must therefore be shown by the troops; and if a despicable individual should be found capable of inflicting a wanton injury or insult on any Cherokee man, woman or child, it is hereby made the special duty of the nearest good officer or man instantly to interpose, and to seize and consign the guilty wretch to the severest penalty of the law . . . .

"Now look at this one." Miss Biddie handed another paper to Artemas. It was General Scott's order to the Cherokees dated May 17, 1838:

> CHEROKEES: The President of the U.S. has sent me, with a powerful army, to cause you, in obedience to the treaty of 1835, to join that part of your people who are already established in prosperity on the other side of the Mississippi . . . .
>
> I am come to carry out that determination. My troops already occupy many positions in the country that you are to abandon, and thousands are approaching from every quarter, to render assistance and escape is hopeless.
>
> Think of this, my Cherokee brethren! I am an old warrior, and have been present at many a scene of slaughter; so spare me, I beseech you . . . .

Miss Biddie was now coming to the end of her tragic story. "Scott's troops began rounding up the Cherokees and placing them in makeshift stockades exactly two years after the Removal Treaty became effective. With the help of the Georgia Guard, the Cherokees were arrested in their homes and fields and were allowed to take only belongings they could carry to the place of confinement. No effort was made to identify or keep families together, and husbands and wives and parents and children were often separated and placed in different stockades. White mobs followed the troops, looting the abandoned Cherokee homes and villages and even their graves. Hundreds died in the stockades before the westward trip ever began. It was inevitable, and Chief John Ross finally agreed to lead the exodus, and $65.88 per person was appropriated to finance the trip."

Artemas could tell that it was getting painful for Miss Biddie to continue, but she was determined to tell this last part herself. "Severe drought made river travel impossible. So 13,000 Cherokees of the main body were moved overland in a 645-wagon train that began at Murphy, North Carolina, the last of October 1838. This was late in the fall, and they wound their way through the five states of Tennessee, Kentucky, Illinois, Missouri, and Arkansas during the most bitter cold winter months. They arrived at Tallaquah in what is now the state of Oklahoma about five months later on March 26, 1839."

Miss Biddie had saved one last document, which she held with a trembling hand. It was from a soldier, John G. Burnett, who later rose to the rank of colonel in the Confederate Army.

One can never forget the sadness and solemnity of that morning. We started west. Chief John Ross led in prayer and when the bugle sounded and the wagons started rolling many of the children rose to their feet and waved their little hand good-bye to their mountain homes, knowing they were leaving forever. Many of these helpless people did not have blankets and many of them had been driven from their home bare-footed.

On the morning of November the 17th we encountered a ter-rific sleet and snow storm with freezing temperatures and from that day until we reached the end of the fateful journey on March 26, 1839, the sufferings of the Cherokees were awful. The trail of the exiles was a trail of death. They had to sleep in the wagons and on the ground without fire. And I have known as many as 22 of them to die in one night of pneumonia due to ill treatment, cold and exposure. Among this number was the beautiful Christian wife of Chief John Ross. This noble hearted woman died a martyr to childhood, giving her only blanket for the protection of a sick child . . . .

I wish I could forget it all, but the picture of suffering humanity still lingers in my memory.

No one said anything when Artemas finished reading until Miss Biddie broke the silence. "So why am I here, I guess you are asking. Well not all of the Cherokees made the trip. Many of those living in North Carolina got exempted by their white legal counsel, William Thomas, and they were allowed to remain in return for their acceptance of the sovereignty of the state of North Carolina over their villages. They were joined later by other Cherokees who escaped General Scott's dragnet by hiding out in the mountains, about a thousand of them.

"Chief Tsali, or Charley, as some called him, became a hero as the highest-ranking Cherokee leader to resist the removal. General Scott decided to make an example of him after he and his followers killed several soldiers while trying to escape the roundup and hid out in the hills. Tsali and all but the youngest of his sons agreed to surrender and be executed in return for the pledge of General Scott that the remainder of their band would be allowed to remain unmolested in North Carolina."

Elder Thomas brought the lesson to an end. "There was continuing strife between Cherokee leaders who accepted and those who opposed the removal, and most of those who accepted met violent deaths, including Elias Boudinot, who was assassinated. John Ross continued as principal chief for decades."

Artemas had not touched his tea and had remained still as this story of Miss Biddie's people sank in. He would never forget it and would retell it time and time again as he moved from one ministry to another in the coming years.

CHAPTER 5

God's Amazing Handiwork

Too quickly the day came for Artemas "to go on over the mountain," as the Elder put it. By now he was used to his old mule, Beulah. "She ain't a racking horse like David Crockett had where people would come from miles around just to watch its gait, but Beulah is gentle and sure footed," Mr. Wimpy had told him. "She's a good'un and mules eat less than horses do and their feet ain't brittle. A mule is careful; it ain't stubborn. They just think about what's happening to them and to you, and that's what you're going to need going over that mountain by yourself."

One could get into Union County from Lumpkin by many different routes, through Frogtown Gap, Woody Gap, Cooper Gap, Grassy Gap, Hightower Gap, and Ward's Gap, but not all had good trails. Frogtown Gap was named because of the Cherokees' legend that once a big frog, "Walasiyi," hopped around the mountains. Blood and Slaughter mountains were named for a fierce battle where the Creeks were encroaching on Cherokee territory and were defeated and turned back. On Blood Mountain was a cave said to run fifty feet through solid rock into the mountain. As Miss Biddie had told, Cherokee legend was that it was the home of the Yunwee Chuns Dee, little people who could fly and make magic music.

The conventional wisdom in Dahlonega was that Artemas should use the Logan Turnpike and go through Tesnatee or Wild Turkey Gap. It was the oldest and best route; "been there for years, steep but well marked," they said.

The Elder had assured Artemas that he did not have to get his provisions in Dahlonega, that it would be better to wait until he got to the Tate Store run by two brothers, John and Thomas. The Tesnatee Gap road was about ten or twelve miles from Dahlonega. "They can give you the latest," was how he put it. "They know the lay of the land

and what's been coming and going in recent days. I'll see you when you come back through. God bless you," the Elder said and sent Artemas on his way.

"Good thing you're going in the winter. It'll be colder than a well digger's ears, but them rattlesnakes won't be crawling," the storekeeper, Thomas Tate, told Artemas as he helped him load up the supplies. "A couple of years ago, a fellow, I think his name was Helton, killed a big one right in the middle of the trail, cut it in half with his axe, and when he went to examine the part with the head on it, it bit him and nearly killed him. Ever heard of such a thing?"

Shortly after Union County had been created in the early 1830s, the Union Turnpike Company got a state charter to build a toll road across Tesnatee Gap. It was completed in 1840 and was used heavily by Union County farmers taking their goods to market in Cleveland, Clermont, and Gainesville. General James Longstreet had moved to Gainesville in 1875, thinking it would become the new railroad hub of the South. In 1841, Major Francis Logan bought the rights to run the toll road into Union County and built a house, an inn or "house of entertainment" as it was then called, and a toll gate. Thirty years later in 1871, Logan purchased land on the north end of the road in Union County, and that was when it became known as the Logan Turnpike.

Although it was in the middle of winter and the mountains were grey and stark, Artemas could feel the magic of their grandeur. He had no way of knowing it at the time, but these ancient, rugged mountains had 2,000 kinds of plants, 130 species of trees, 150 species of nesting birds, and 150 kinds of salamanders. Years before, buffalo and elk had roamed these mountains, and in 1885, as Artemas made his trip, there were still wolves, foxes, panthers, and bears. Thomas Tate had told him that a beaver weighing 69 pounds had been killed near the turnpike only a few weeks before Artemas came by. Native brook trout were abundant. It was some of God's earliest and most amazing handiwork.

And it had taken God a while to perfect it. Almost 250 million years earlier, the earth's crust had buckled and folded into mountains. Known as the Alleghenian Orogemy, or the Appalachian Revolution, it created vast deposits of fossil fuels throughout Appalachia, some 63,000 square miles of bituminous coal beds, it was later learned. Then began millions of years of eroding and leveling, bringing 30,000-foot-high mountains down to 6,000 feet or less. Finally, what was produced and what Artemas was riding through were the beautiful, soon-to-be green, flowering mountains that extend from the Gaspe' Peninsula of Quebec to northern Alabama. They reach their zenith in the great Blue Ridge, rising south of Harrisburg, Pennsylvania, and continuing as both one main axis and divided ranges into North Georgia. It is the world's largest, most varied, and probably first deciduous forest. And it is where Artemas found himself that cold January day in 1885.

At the time of the Appalachian Revolution, the Arctic was warmer and the continents joined across Alaska and the North Pole. Beginning some 70 million years before Artemas made his trek, a vast circumpolar forest developed across that bridge with plants moving both to and from Eurasia and North America. The result is that many trees and flowers in parts of China are the same as in Appalachia.

Back then, the Rockies were mere foothills, and the peaks of Appalachia towered over those of the Alps. Then, further movements within the earth separated the continents and 25 million years ago produced the rugged mountain chain extending from Canada to New Mexico that is the Rockies of today. The rise of those new peaks and ridges cut off moisture from the west, rendered the central part of the continent too dry to support trees, and pushed the forest eastward to the point where it could thrive on rain carried inland from the Atlantic.

The Arctic turned cold about a million years ago, and massive glaciers thousands of feet thick were spread across the northern landscape. The ice extended into what is now Pennsylvania and Ohio, and its force bulldozed the forests it covered like a giant earthmover. Fortunately, the North American Mountains ranged from north to south, and the displaced trees retreated before the flow of ice rather than being crushed by it as they were against the east-to-west ranges in Europe. That is how they survived to reestablish themselves on the receptive slopes and in the fertile valleys and isolated coves of

Southern Appalachia. Ecologists classified it as a "mixed mesophytic forest," and lumbermen spoke of it as "cove hardwoods." Artemas just knew it was spectacular.

The spruces, firs, and other conifers occupied the high ridges and peaks of the southern mountains, and the broad-leafed hardwoods with their storehouse of seeds thrived in the protected valleys and coves. Southward from the Cumberland Valley evolved into "a master experiment station." Artemas was in the heart of it where the number of species of trees was greater by 50 percent than that found in any other location on earth, all growing in mutual and beneficial coexistence. There was never a more varied deciduous forest anywhere or at any time.

As the climate reversed itself, the hardier of the species followed the retreating ice and replanted the devastated regions with trees that could survive in the changed soil and weather environment. That is why the New England heights became predominately coniferous with spruces and firs on or near the summits and pines and hemlocks down the slopes. The forests from the Catskills southward became increasingly deciduous until the seasonal trees, which flower in spring and flame in fall, predominated the highlands of the Carolinas, Tennessee, and Georgia.

Even though the young preacher had none of this information, he did not need a book to tell him he was in a special place in God's great universe. It was in these coves of Southern Appalachia that all the varieties met, flowered, and prospered. The oaks reached a diameter of five to six feet. Chestnut trees, which made up one-fourth of all the trees in the Appalachian forest when Artemas came through, grew from six to nine feet across, and tulip poplars grew even thicker than that and often eighty feet to the nearest limb.

Botanist William Bartram, on his plant-hunting trips into the Southern Appalachian Mountains, discovered the azalea and spread its fame throughout the world as "the most gay and brilliant flowering shrub yet known." Artemas would marvel at them a few months later in the spring. Renowned naturalist John Muir summed it up with his observation that the Appalachian forests "must have been a great delight to God; for they were the best He ever planted."

The mountains and trees of the Southern Appalachians had achieved their finished grandeur long before the first white man got a glimpse of them. Wholly unlike the raw, rugged, and barren peaks of the Alps, Andes, Himalayas, and Rockies, they are, with few exceptions, rounded and forested with few commanding peaks.

Most of the high points are in the 3,000-foot range, but there are several higher. The tallest is Mount Mitchell in North Carolina, which stands at 6,685 feet and is clothed in spruce and fir. A close second is Clingmans Dome at 6,642 feet. Eight peaks in Georgia exceed 4,000 feet, the highest being Brasstown Bald at 4,784 feet above sea level. Rabun Bald is only a few feet lower at 4,711.

Because the trees shed their foliage in autumn and are reclothed in new dress in spring, two major byproducts of the Southern Appalachian woodlands are the masses of wildflowers in spring and the dazzling colors of the changing leaves in fall. Artemas would get to see violets, anemones, hepaticas, phloxes, lilies, trilliums, and myriad other seasonal flowers burst forth when the warm sun of March and April struck Brasstown Valley.

As many as thirty of the trees among cove hardwoods bear handsome blossoms with flowering periods extending from the snowy-white blooms of serviceberry in March to the yellow flowers of the witch-hazel in December. Flowering plants of tree proportions would include redbud, magnolia, tulip poplar, buckeye, dogwood, locust, crabapple, mountain ash, black haw, yellowwood, fringe-tree, silver bell, lindens, sourwood, and Hercules-club. And in the borders between the trees and the shrubs are the rhododendron, mountain laurel, and those azaleas that grow in profusion.

Fall coloring differs from Northern to Southern Appalachia, with the maples and birches blazing in New England in early October and the vivid colors of the hardwoods and sourwoods progressing down the spine of the great Blue Ridge through early November. This is a time when the sweet gum of the Deep South are still flaunting their scarlet, purple, and gold.

A continuing mystery to ecologists and naturalists alike are the eighty or so grassy islands called balds that are found 4,000 feet and higher in the saddles between the forested peaks from Virginia to

Georgia. Artemas would see Mount Enotah, later to be called Brasstown Bald, the following day when he went through Testnatee Gap. These balds were used as summer grazing lands when settlers first arrived in the mountains, and, although it has been suggested that they may have been either caused by lightning or cleared by Indians as places of worship, no concrete explanation has been offered for these lush alpine pastures. They are made even more intriguing by the fact that the cinquefoil, a member of the rose family that is a native of the Gaspesian Highlands of Quebec, is also native to these balds. The same snow buntlings that feed on its wine-red seed capsules in Canada do the same on those of Southern Appalachia.

Further mysteries of the coves are the varieties of orchid species and exotic ferns. They are throwbacks to climates and geologic eras lost in the dim pasts of prehistoric times.

Such were the mountains in which Artemas, all alone except for Beulah, found himself with no one to talk to. But it gave him time to think of what had brought him there. Ever since that life-changing night in Yatesville with Reverend Hamby, Artemas would think of the questions he had been asked. One that continued to concern Artemas was "Why are you a Methodist?" And before Artemas could stutter an attempt at an answer, Hamby had moved on to how and when he would talk to Presiding Elder Thomas in Dahlonega. But it was a good question, and Artemas knew he needed a good answer. He remembered that John Wesley had once defined "a true Methodist" as one who has "the love of God shed abroad in his heart by the Holy Spirit."

Artemas had once read that John Wesley on his deathbed called out, "Where is my sermon on the Love of God? Take it and spread it about. Give it to everyone." The local Methodist preacher in Yatesville had allowed Artemas to borrow his copy of some of Wesley's letters and writings. Parts of them he had read more than once, and he remembered Wesley's doctrine of Christian perfection was "to love God with all one's heart and soul and mind, and to love one's neighbor as one's self." *More study and experience is needed,* he decided as he and Beulah made their way along the trail.

With a huge rhododendron slick on each side, Artemas dismounted and stretched his aching back and squatted a few times, flexing his stiff legs. He had been on his mule only about three hours, and he still had most of the day to go. His rear was sore no matter how he shifted his body around in the saddle. He could not help wondering how the Wesley brothers had ridden year after year, day after day. How had Francis Asbury done it and the hundreds of other horseback-riding preachers who had endured this kind of discomfort to spread the gospel? He thought of Peter Cartwright, converted at sixteen, who preached more than 15,000 sermons over 53 years and conducted 500 funerals.

Asbury had been the first Methodist Appalachian circuit rider. Breaking with his friend and mentor John Wesley who supported the British in the Revolutionary War, Asbury had taken the side of the colonies and became the leader of Methodism in the new country. It was he who took the Methodist religion into the frontier, preaching wherever he could find an audience from 300 to 500 sermons a year. Artemas shook his head in amazement as he remembered that Asbury had ridden more than 270,000 miles on horseback, more than anyone who ever lived except the Wesleys themselves. He had crossed the Appalachian Mountains sixty times. Even when he couldn't stand to preach the last seven years of his ministry, Asbury still rode. Ashamed of his own weakness, Artemas, not even two days on the road, got back on his mule and contritely continued on his way.

The trail seemed to be almost straight up as it neared the gap, "steep as a horse's face," Elder Thomas had described it. Artemas got off his horse the last couple of miles and led the animal up the steep 40-degree slope. But when he got to the gap and could look into the vistas of the Blue Ridge, it was worth it. Artemas Lester from the flatlands of middle Georgia looked down into the Nottley River Valley, the Turkey Pen Flats, and over at the summit of Mount Enotah. Artemas found the descent down into Lordamercy Cove was just as steep as coming up, and again he dismounted Beulah along the rocky wet path. Artemas would later learn that the wagon drivers would cut a large sapling and drag it behind the wagon to slow it on the down slope.

The magnificent trees continued, and as he neared the bottom of the mountain white frozen springheads seeped into the road from each side. He was in Choestoe Valley. After about a mile the small branches became a creek known as Town Creek, and then for the first time in two days he saw signs of civilization. Fields had been cleared and small pastures appeared. When Thompson Collins, one of the first settlers to come through Tesnatee Gap into the new county, saw this rolling land in 1832, he knew it was what he had been looking for. His search was over. This was where he and Celia Self Collins would raise their ten children. There he stopped and there he would stay until his death in 1858.

Reverend Hamby had given Elder Thomas instructions for Artemas to find his home in Owl Town, a good half-day's ride after coming down through Lordamercy Cove. Artemas made it in time for a quick visit to Shady Grove Methodist Church and cemetery and then supper, enjoying for the first time in his life some squirrel and dumplings. After the main meal, Reverend Hamby poured sorghum syrup on a hunk of fresh butter and proceeded to mash and stir it all up together like cake batter. Then he took a big biscuit, broke it in half, and dipped it into the mixture. "Try it, son, you'll like it," Mrs. Hamby urged. Artemas ended up eating two big fluffy biscuits with his syrup and butter. "Cat-head biscuits," the preacher called them, "'cause they're big as a cat's head."

Artemas loved Mrs. Hamby immediately. Her husband called her "Nellie," and Artemas learned she was the sister of two of the best-known preachers in the mountains: Thomas Coke Hughes and John Wesley Hughes. He could see she was the perfect mate for an itinerate preacher gone most of the time with a family to raise much on her own. He hoped he could find a wife like that someday. Artemas and the reverend read passages aloud from their Bibles and then turned in for the night. Right before he blew out the lamp, Reverend Hamby had Artemas promise that he would come back when school started and "see what Bud Miller is doing at Auburn." Artemas would learn that "Bud" was a common nickname in the mountains and was a term of endearment.

CHAPTER 6

Through Track Rock Gap

On a cold winter morning far from home, Artemas woke up tired. Wrestling all night with the devil would do that to you, he knew. As usual with these bouts, he remembered the story his mother had told him when he was a young boy. Funny, he thought, how that short two-minute conversation twenty years ago had stuck with him. So many of the other memories had blurred with time. He remembered how he had once told his mother a fib, a harmless little white lie about why he was late getting his chores done.

She took it seriously and told him it was wrong to lie. "That's Satan pulling at you," she said. "You have to be strong and fight his temptations off for the rest of your life." This is what he remembered the most: "When you know it's Satan tempting you to do something wrong, just say to him—you can do it under your breath—'Get behind me Satan.' That's what the Bible says to do."

Then she kind of smiled to herself and added, "And don't be like your Uncle Donald when he was a little boy. Your grandmother had told him not to go swimming in the creek, and then one afternoon he came in with his hair wet, and she knew he had disobeyed her. 'Didn't I tell you not to go swimming?' she demanded. 'Didn't I tell you that when you're tempted to say, "Get behind me Satan"?' 'I did, Mother,' was his reply, 'and he pushed me in.'"

Artemas still remembered that story, as he had spent the night tossing and turning and wishing he had never left Yatesville, that he had never even met Reverend Hamby, that he was going on a "wild goose chase," another term his mother often used for something frivolous. And he knew that was Satan tempting him to go back home, pulling at him to forget this dream of being a circuit rider and starting a school in these isolated Georgia mountains.

"Get behind me, Satan," Artemas said out loud to the still darkened room, as he pulled on his pants and his boots, ready to face the day.

Artemas was in the saddle and on the trail as day broke. He wanted to get an early start and be in Brasstown Valley by midday. He had known next to nothing about Choestoe until he got there. But one of the sights he would see today was one he had read about in the Elder's book, *Letters from the Alleghany Mountains,* written in 1849 by Charles Lanman.

The author had told about his trip through the Blue Ridge Mountains, through Tesnatee Gap and Lordamercy Cove and into the Choestoe Valley. It was the same route Artemas had taken the day before. Like Artemas, Lanman had come through Dahlonega, and there he had heard about a native wonder called "Track Rock" on the northwestern side of the Blue Ridge Mountains. His curiosity excited, he decided to visit this natural or artificial wonder on foot.

> My course lay over a very uneven country, which was entirely uncultivated, excepting some half dozen quiet vales, which presented a cheerful appearance. The woods were generally composed of oak and chestnut, and destitute to a considerable extent of undergrowth; the soil was composed of clay and sand, and apparently fertile, and clear sparkling brooks intersected the country, and were the first that I had seen in Georgia. I had a number of extensive mountain views, which were more beautiful than imposing.

Lanman had spent the night in Choestoe and related he had been "most hospitably entertained." His host had a family of nine sons and three daughters, not one of whom had ever been out of the wilderness region of Georgia. He found the father was a "very intelligent man by nature, had received no education, and could hardly read a chapter in the Bible." Artemas's interest had been peaked further when he read that the mountain man deeply regretted his inability to give his children the schooling he felt they needed. "I have always desired," said he, "that I could live on some public road, so that my girls might occasionally see a civilized man, since it is fated that they will never meet with that in society."

Lanman felt sorry for the man and tried to direct his attention from himself to the beautiful surrounding country. The old man responded that the mountains could be cultivated to their summits, and that the principle productions of his farm were corn, wheat, rye, and potatoes. He also explained that the country abounded in game, such as deer, turkeys, bears, and an occasional panther. The streams, he said, were well supplied with "large minnows"; Lanman ascertained he meant the brook trout.

Lanman wrote that while he was talking with the man, they were startled by the baying of his hounds, and on looking up the Tesnatee Gap road saw a fine-looking doe coming toward them on the run.

> In its terror the poor creature made a sudden turn, and scaling a garden fence was overtaken by the dogs on a spot near which the wife of the man was planting seeds. She immediately seized a pole, and by a single blow deprived the doe of life. In a very few moments, her husband was on the ground, and, with his knife slit the throat of the animal. They then re-entered their dwelling as if nothing had happened out of the common order of events.

Lanman recorded that it was the first deer that he had ever known to be killed by a woman, and when he complimented his friend on the dogs, the man bragged that one of them was a "powerful runner" and had been known to follow a deer for three days and three nights.

Then he remarked that they were "very plenty" of snakes in the region and, like the mountaineer Artemas had met at the Turnpike entrance, had a snake story to tell.

> I saw a snake fight between a black-racer and a rattlesnake. It was in the road, about a mile from here, and when I saw them, the racer had the other by the back of the head, and was coiling his body all around him as if to squeeze him to death. The scuffle was pretty severe, but the racer soon killed the fellow with rattles, and I killed the racer. It was a queer scrape, and I reckon you do not often see the like in your country.

On the following day, Lanman visited "the Mecca of my pilgrimage, and was—disappointed." He explained it this way: "This is Track Rock, and it's no great shakes after all."

> I found it occupying an unobtrusive place by the roadside. It is off an irregular form and quite smooth, rises gradually from the ground to the height of perhaps three feet, and is about twenty feet long by the most liberal measurements. It is evidently covered with a great variety of tracks, including those of men, bears or dogs, and turkeys, together with indistinct impressions of a man's hand. Some of the impressions are half an inch thick, while many of them appear to be almost entirely effaced. The rock seems to be a species of slate colored soapstone. The conclusion to which I have arrived, after careful examination, is as follows: This rock is located on what was once an Indian trail, and, having been used by the Cherokees as a resting place, it was probably their own ingenuity which conceived and executed the characters which now puzzle the philosophy of many men. The scenery about Track Rock is not remarkable for its grandeur, though you can hardly turn the eye in any direction without beholding an agreeable mountain landscape.

Artemas was not aware of it at the time, but eighteen years after Lanman in 1867, another notable writer had passed through the same route and observed the same rock. His name was John Muir, and he was on one of his first "rambles," as he called them. Muir had started in Louisville, Kentucky, and before it was over he would walk a thousand miles to Cedar Keys, Florida. When Muir came through "Track Gap" as he called it, he was twenty-nine, the same age as Artemas. The great naturalist would later "ramble" and explore the Grand Canyon, Yosemite, Mount Rainer, the Petrified Forest, and Glacier Bay, Alaska, just to name a few.

Muir always kept a journal, and from his notes it was obvious that he was partial to the Appalachian Mountains. Writing about them, he said he was "eager to baptize all my fellow sinners in the beauty of God's Mountains." Although Artemas had not read this description by

Muir, he was thinking the exact same words. *God's Mountains*, Artemas thought as he too was being "baptized" in their beauty.

Muir had arrived there by making his way from Knoxville, Tennessee, to the Ocoee River and then east to Murphy, North Carolina. There he stayed a few days with a family in Murphy and then traveled the Hiawassee River upstream to one of its tributaries, Brasstown Creek, and then on into Brasstown Valley, the same path that Artemas was taking in reverse. On September 22, 1867, he detailed that part of his long trip this way:

> About noon I reached the last mountain summit on my way to the sea. It is called the Blue Ridge and before it lies a prospect very different from any I had passed, namely, a vast uniform expanse of dark pine woods, extending to the sea; an impressive view at any time and under any circumstances, but particularly so to one emerging from the mountains . . . . I reached Yonah Mountain in the evening. Had a long conversation with an old Methodist slaveholder and mine owner. He was very hospitable. I refreshed with a drink of cider.

During this trip Muir wrote friends back home saying his route would be through Blairsville and Gainesville, Georgia, and to please write him at Gainesville. "I am terribly lonely. I hardly dare think of home and friends."

On another day, he wrote of the Master's hand: "Oh, these vast, calm, measureless mountain days . . . in whose light everything seems equally divine, opening a thousand windows to show us God."

And at this journey's end he concluded, "Of the people of the states that I have now passed, I best like the Georgians."

Artemas made it to the low gap of the famous rock shortly before noon. He had not hurried and had only stopped once to let the horse rest and relieve himself. Mostly he drank in the spectacular beauty of the mountain vista as had Muir and Lanman before him. Near the rock he had noticed a narrow trail wandering off to his right through thick laurel thickets that the natives called "Laurel Hells." One had to get down on all fours to crawl through them; they were so dense and thick. He later learned this was a steep trail of about six miles to the summit of Mount Enotah, later called Brasstown Bald. "Brasstown," he had already learned, was a misinterpretation of the Cherokee Indian word "Itse' yi," which means "town of the green valley" or a "place made green with vegetation." The early exploring white men confused it with another Cherokee word, "Untsai yi," which sounds similar and translates "brass." When and who made the misinterpretation is not known, for no one likes admitting a mistake, Artemas mused to himself. So when the valley was first surveyed in 1828, the valley and the creek were called Brasstown.

Track Rock was a disappointment to Artemas in 1885 just as it had for Lanman in 1849 and Muir in 1867, and doubtless would be to many in the future. Obviously it had held more allure, even some superstition, Artemas supposed, for the Cherokees who called it "Datori nasgun yi" or "where there are tracks."

At that time, little did Artemas know just how long human beings had inhabited that area. More than 10,000 years before, human beings were living in what would become Brasstown Valley. They lived on hillsides and ridge tops overlooking rivers much larger then Brasstown Creek, which Artemas would soon cross.

Approximately 6,000 years later, the climate in the region that would become the southeast stabilized to the current temperate conditions. Brasstown Valley was then formed some 4,000 years before by what became known as Brasstown Creek, a tributary to the Hiawassee River, which is in turn a tributary of the Tennessee River. Then nuts, fruits, and berries became available. Trees provided building material and fuel for fire. Cane along the creek bank would be used for baskets and mats. Mammals would provide meat, bone, hide, and fur. Human habitation improved.

The historic period began when the Spanish explorer Hernando de Soto reached what became Georgia in the spring of 1540 with 600 men, 243 horses, and several hundred hogs. He had sailed from Cuba to Tampa Bay and then into Georgia. Much is known of this long-ago expedition because a man called the "Gentleman from Elvas" (a town in Portugal) kept a well-written and detailed journal.

As a young man, de Soto had come to Panama and helped Pizarro conquer the Incas in Peru in 1531. For that, de Soto's share was $100,000 in gold. And he wanted more. He would spend the rest of his life trying to find it.

It is known that de Soto explored the Fall Line area of the Flint River (where Artemas Lester would be born about 310 years later), then continued on to the Ocmulgee River area, and then traveled northward, probably veering to the west. There is some uncertainty of this route, and there are those who claim he was in the Nacoochee Valley area in northeast Georgia. It is known with certainty that he spent six days in the Cartersville/Rome area trading with the Indians, getting into a fight with them, and taking some of them as slaves and hostages. As he continued on, he probably went into the area of Chattanooga, down into Alabama, then west until he crossed the Mississippi River and spent much of 1541 exploring Arkansas. Wherever de Soto went, he treated the Indians harshly and brought contagious diseases that killed many of them. He died from a fever in May 1542. His men, not wanting the Indians to know their leader was dead, buried him in a box filled with sand and sunk in it the Mississippi River somewhere in Louisiana. When what was left of de Soto's 600-man army reached Mexico the next year, only 40 men and 22 horses remained. A rough map survived from the expedition in the mountain area they had traveled, and the area was listed as "Appalachee."

As stated, it is unlikely that de Soto came over the big mountains into the area of Brasstown Valley or into the area only a few miles away where the gold he was looking for would be found nearly 300 years later. It is known that by 1750 there were three tiers of Cherokee settlements: Upper, Middle, and Lower. The Cherokee areas were Nanqucchee (Nacoochee), Cholee, and Cuttacoche and then there was Tasache near the headwaters of the Hiawassee River not far from Brasstown Valley.

There were Indian villages in Brasstown Valley in the 1500s. Their patterns along Brasstown Creek consisted of what were called winter and summer houses situated close together, a burial plot, and a joint area for processing, cooking, and storing food. There were also pits for trash at each end of the village.

Artemas sat on a rock in "Appalachee" and ate a biscuit and the side meat he had brought with him. He then continued down the trail to his destination. After less than an hour, the trail dead-ended into a wider rutted wagon trail that he could see crossed Brasstown Creek on his right. A small log building was on a nearby hill to his left with a hitching post outside. This was the Track Rock Post Office. Artemas had given the Methodist church officials this address as his destination. A Mr. Butt, whom Artemas assumed was the postmaster, greeted him warmly, especially after he learned he was the circuit-riding Methodist preacher they had heard was coming.

"We've been looking for you," he said, as if Artemas was late to his assignment. But when Artemas told him about his stops in Dahlonega and Choestoe, he seemed more understanding and wanted to ask about some acquaintances there. "Did you get to Blairsville?" he asked, and on learning that Artemas hadn't, urged him to do so when he had time. "It's back this way," he pointed to the rutted red mud wagon road behind him. "You need to look up Tom Harralson, Thomas Jefferson Harralson, that is; he runs the Tan Yard; he runs Blairsville. And Doc Rogers." The postmaster was a talker, Artemas could see. "Have you met Thomas Coke Hughes?" Without giving Artemas time to answer, he continued, "You talk about an exhorter. He is the best I've heard. We call him the 'Bishop of the Mountains.' And he's got a brother 'bout as good, John Wesley Hughes." When Artemas told him he had spent the night with Reverend Hamby, he said, "Oh, well, you met their sister Nellie." Then he started raving about Reverend Hamby's exhorting ability. Artemas made a mental note to make it a point to look up both the Reverend Hughes and Mr. Harralson; they sounded like people worth knowing.

Thomas Coke, for whom the Union County man was obviously named, had been one of John Wesley's top assistants in Methodism. In fact, he, more than anyone in that day, was responsible for spreading Methodism beyond the English-speaking world. Wesley had thought Coke was too impatient, too impulsive, and that often he assumed more authority than Wesley wanted to give him. But Coke, with the help of Asbury, had formed Cokesbury College and finally, after years of pleading, had persuaded the Methodists to let him go on a missionary expedition to India. He died on board a ship before he got there, and Artemas remembered the story was that Coke's body was found kneeling in prayer in his cabin. *Yes,* Artemas thought, *I'd like to meet this man's namesake. Up here in these mountains, a Methodist preacher named for Thomas Coke!* He still could not get over how learned and civilized many of these mountain people were.

It was hard to finish a conversation with Postmaster Butt. It seemed he loved meeting strangers coming through the trail; there were too few of them. "I'm going on down to the settlement," Artemas finally said, mounting his mule and heading across the creek that he figured was the Union-Towns County Line.

"That first house you're going to come to," Butt had explained, "is the old Bryson place. It's been here a spell. John Bryson came into this valley right when the Indians were being sent out west in the '30s. There was a stockade not far from this house. He was one of Union County's first legislators. There's a bunch of Brysons in this valley, you'll see. Mrs. Bryson still lives there with one of her sons, Mangum, but she's been bad off for a spell."

CHAPTER 7

"The New Georgia"

At this time in the 1880s, the state of Georgia was filled with notable leaders. The terrible days of war and Reconstruction were over, and things looked brighter. Atlanta had again become the center of economic life, and a new capitol building was being constructed. One and a half million people lived in the state, and Georgia had more miles of railroad than any state except Texas. In the year 1880, more than a million bales of cotton and a million dollars' worth of gold came out of Georgia, coal mining was a growing industry, and marble had become important. It was of such high grade that the French sculptor, Daniel Chester French, used forty tons of Georgia marble to carve the marvelous statue of Lincoln in the memorial in Washington. Granite in Elbert County was beginning to be mined.

Agriculture was on its way to a new prosperity with commercial fertilizer coming into use. Textile mills flourished with the number of factories doubling and output tripling within a decade. Clay for bricks was proving to be profitable. Naval stores and timber were increasingly important, and sawmills were springing up most everywhere.

U.S. senator Benjamin H. Hill described the time as "one of those rare junctures in human affairs where one civilization ends and another begins."

But no such prosperity had spread to the Georgia mountains. In a couple more decades, sawmills and lumber barons would come and strip the timber from the mountains that Muir and Bartram had raved about. And a deadly pestilence about that time would kill the huge chestnut trees that were everywhere when Artemas traveled the mountain trails.

Henry W. Grady had become known as the "Spokesman for the New South." His ancestors named "O'Grady" had come from Ireland, then through North Carolina into Mountain Town near Ellijay,

Georgia, and then into Athens where Henry was born. So when Henry gave his famous speech about a Pickens County funeral, he knew well what he was talking about.

In 1886, Grady carried his message to New York City, where he talked of the old Georgia and the new Georgia, and as he had so many times before, he told the Pickens County funeral story. His speech about a dead man dramatically focused attention on Georgia's need to manufacture its own products and not let its raw materials be sent out of the state to make richer the owners of factories in the North. This is what he said:

> I attended a funeral in a Georgia county. It was a poor, one-gallused fellow. They buried him in the midst of a marble quarry; yet the little tombstone they put above him was from Vermont. They buried him in the midst of a pine forest, but his pine coffin was imported from Cincinnati. They buried him within the touch of an iron mine, but the nails in his coffin and the iron in the shovel that dug his grave were from Pittsburgh. They buried him near the best sheep grazing county in the world, yet the wool in the coffin bands was brought from the North. They buried him in a New York coat, a Boston pair of shoes, a pair of breeches from Chicago, and a shirt from Cincinnati. Georgia furnished only the corpse and a hole in the ground.

Interestingly, General William T. Sherman was there, and Grady chastised him for "being a little careless with fire." He went on to say, however, that "from those ashes you left in 1864 we have built a brave and beautiful city in Atlanta. We have caught the sunshine in the bricks and mortar of our homes and have built therein not one ignoble prejudice or memory." Sherman was impressed with the young Georgia speaker.

Three years later Grady would catch a cold that would turn into pneumonia and kill him at the age of thirty-nine. He would be buried on Christmas Day 1889. While he was alive, Grady had helped promote expositions to show off the state. The biggest one was in 1881 when the Liberty Bell was brought from Philadelphia and more than a million visitors came to view Georgia products and meet the leading citizens.

There were dozens of fascinating political figures in Georgia during this period. Some had been leaders before and during the Civil War and then continued their leadership into the last quarter of the nineteenth century, such as Joseph E. Brown, John B. Gordon, Alexander H. Stephens, Robert Toombs, and Thomas E. Watson.

Joseph E. Brown dominated Georgia politics for four decades, most of that time serving as U.S. senator and governor. Born in poverty near Pickens, South Carolina, in 1823, he moved as a boy to Gaddistown in what would later become Union County. At nineteen, he walked a yoke of steers to Calhoun Academy in South Carolina. There he traded the steers for eight months of schooling. An excellent scholar, he tutored the children of a physician to continue his education right through Yale Law School.

Joseph E. Brown

Returning to Georgia, he set up a law practice in Cherokee County and was soon elected to the state senate and later judge of the Blue Ridge Circuit. He was in his wheat field working when he learned that the Democratic Party had nominated him to run for governor against American Party candidate Benjamin Harvey Hill. It was a fascinating contest. Hill was the greatest orator of his day; Brown was awkward, almost tongue-tied. Most considered

Alexander H. Stephens

it would be a one-sided election. However, the silver-tongued Hill made the mistake of referring to Brown as "slow" and making fun of a quilt that a group of mountain women had presented him as a campaign contribution. The newspapers took up the cause of the quilt; one in Milledgeville editorialized, "Hurrah for the girls of Cherokee, the plough boy judge and the calico quilt."

Brown established himself with the common people by responding, "I'm a slow man and proud of it. Any man who holds in his hands the destinies of his people must be cautious and slow to act." No darker horse in any campaign ever won a greater victory. Brown got 10,000 more votes than Hill in an election where about 100,000 voted.

Brown proved to be a dynamo as soon as he took office, taking on the banks and advocating that rentals from the state-owned railroad be earmarked for education. A strong states-righter, he expanded and reformed the state militia, making Georgia the best prepared of the Confederate States when the Civil War erupted. His followers called him "Young Hickory" because he reminded them of the rustic and take-charge Andrew Jackson. He was elected to a second term by a landslide.

He was a secessionist but had reservations about the Confederacy in general and Jefferson Davis in particular. He was a thorn in the Confederate president's side during the entire war. Brown did not want a third term and refused to campaign for one, but he was reelected handily and took the oath of office wearing a suit of Georgia-made jeans. Brown was an organizational genius and a hands-on manager. Every time the Confederacy called up more troops, he'd recruit younger and older Georgians until in the latter days of the war he had a state guard mainly of military school students, including his own son, and old men. When there were no rifles available, he armed them with spears known as "Joe Brown's Pikes." Many of them were made over the mountain from Brasstown Valley in Nacoochee.

In the middle of the war he was elected to a fourth term as governor largely on the strength of Georgia fighting men on the battlefronts. When the war ended, he was arrested and briefly incarcerated in Washington, D.C. President Andrew Johnson then pardoned him after he promised he would resign as governor and advocate citizen acceptance of the war's end and the conditions of Reconstruction.

Because of this action, Brown instantly went from being Georgia's most popular and beloved political figure to its most hated. He was savagely denounced, and when he decided to go to the Republican Convention, he was called a "turncoat" and "opportunist." Reconstruction governor Rufus Bullock appointed him chief justice of the Georgia Supreme Court where he served two years and resigned. He then went into business, railroads, and coalmines and soon became a multi-millionaire.

But his burning ambition was to be vindicated and have his reputation restored with the people. In 1880 when John B. Gordon resigned as U.S. senator, Governor Alfred Colquitt appointed Brown to succeed him in Washington. There he made good use of the position and regained much of the popular acclaim he longed for by leading the fight to defeat legislation that denied Mexican War pensions to those who had fought for the Confederacy. He died in 1884, and a few years later his son "Little Joe" was elected governor.

Alexander H. Stephens, or "Little Aleck" as he was affectionately known, was one of the most beloved Georgians in all its history. When he died, 20,000 people came to view his body as it lay in the rotunda of the new capitol, and 100,000 more lined the streets as the casket was taken to the cemetery. He held the office of vice president of the Confederate States of America, yet as a congressman he had repeatedly called for national unity. Abraham Lincoln loved him and once, after hearing him speak, said, "My old eyes are still wet with tears after listening to 'Little Aleck.'"

As with Governor Brown, his relationship with President Jefferson Davis was like that of oil and water. There was constant contention between the two over such basic matters as conscription, suspension of the writ of habeas corpus, and martial law. On these issues Stephens took progressive positions as opposed to the hard and often dictatorial line of Davis. But because of those differences, Stephens spent most of the last year and a half of the war at his beloved home, Liberty Hall in Crawfordville, Georgia. He did go to Hampton Roads, Virginia, in February 1865 to meet personally with his old friend, President Lincoln, and the secretary of state, William Seward, in an effort to negotiate a peace settlement. Jefferson Davis, however, would not agree with anything, and the conflict was therefore prolonged for another two months.

As with the other leaders of the Southern states, when the war ended Stephens was arrested and thrown into prison, spending six months at Fort Warren in Boston Harbor. General Ulysses S. Grant interceded on his behalf with President Johnson, and he was set free with his promise that he would accept the outcome of the war and work for reconciliation.

The incarceration eroded his already frail health. His hair turned white at the age of fifty-three. He spent his time behind bars working on a two-volume history, *A Constitutional View of the Late War Between the States*, which had widespread sales throughout the world.

While the history brought him some money, he continually was short on resources. His close friend but often critic, Robert Toombs, constantly bailed him out. Stephens was overly generous to anyone who happened by. He had a "Tramp Room" in his home, and anyone in need of room and board could use it. In fact, the latch was on the outside and they could come and go. He helped the youth in his area by sending more than 100 through college. People from everywhere flocked to his doorstep seeking help, advice, or just a friendly greeting, blessing, and usually a piece of pie.

In 1874 he returned to the U.S. House of Representatives and served there until 1882 when he was elected governor. He died after only four months in office, having caught cold in a chilling wind and rain in Savannah while participating in the 150th anniversary of the founding of Georgia. He had always suffered from delicate health and never weighed much over 100 pounds. In his later years he was confined to a wheelchair. He never married, and his half-brother, Linton, who lived with him, cared for him most of that time.

Despite his infirmities and poor health most of his life, he was aggressive in nature and absolutely fearless. He challenged at least three prominent Georgians to duels, including Benjamin Harvey Hill, none of whom granted him satisfaction. He was once knifed badly by a judge who had taken exception to a remark Stephens made about him. The story was that the judge drew a knife on him and demanded an apology. Stephens replied, "Never, cut if you wish," which the judge did.

His colorful character combined with a superior intellect and a devotion to helping others made him one of the most beloved Georgians in the state's history. And that is why Alexander H. Stephens is one of the two Georgians in Statuary Hall in the nation's Capitol.

One story of Stephen's relationship with Robert Toombs says much about the up-and-down relationship these two men had. Once in a debate between the two, Toombs was speaking and Stephens interrupted him. Toombs turned to his diminutive opponent and said, "Shut up, you little runt, or I'll bite your head off." To which "Little Aleck" quickly retorted, "Well, if you did, you'd have more brains in your stomach than you've got in your head."

Robert Toombs had everything that Stephens did not. He was tall, robust, and handsome, with a head of shiny black hair. And he was rich. He was born with both a silver spoon and a silver tongue in his mouth. A hard drinker, his escapades as a student at the University of Georgia twice got him expelled. Legend has it that when his class graduated and he was not part of it, he made a rival commencement speech under an oak tree nearby on the campus. When those at the exercise heard that Toombs was speaking outside, they emptied the hall to go hear him instead of the commencement speaker.

He and Stephens were elected in the same year—1842—to Congress, and in 1853 Toombs was elected to the U.S. Senate. When the Whig Party to which they both belonged split over slavery, they both went into the Democratic Party. They were on opposing sides of the secession question at the Georgia Convention, Toombs strongly for it, arguing, "if war comes we can beat those Yankees with corn-stalks." Stephens opposed secession. But Toombs's oratory carried the day, and Georgia cast its lot with South Carolina in withdrawing from the Union. Toombs then went back to Washington and delivered a fiery resignation speech denouncing the federal government's encroachments upon state sovereignty.

Never a man lacking for confidence in his own abilities, Toombs believed he was best qualified to be president of the Confederacy and was disappointed that Jefferson Davis was chosen. Many thought that if the election had been by individual delegates and not states, Toombs would have been elected.

He became secretary of state, found himself uncomfortable in that position, and resigned to become a general in the Confederate Army. He acquitted himself well at the Battle of Antietam, but had trouble getting along with the other officers. When the war ended, he fled first to Cuba and then to France and England. Unlike the others, he never applied for a pardon and was known as the "Unreconstructed Rebel." When reminded that he had said before the war that the Yankees could be "defeated with cornstalks," he glibly answered, "They wouldn't fight with cornstalks."

When he finally came back to Georgia, he practiced law but could not hold public office. When Little Aleck died, Toombs gave the eulogy and was so overcome that he stood sobbing for five minutes, unable to speak.

His final service to his state was as a member of the Constitutional Convention in 1877 after reconstruction was over. When the state treasury ran out of money to pay the delegates, he offered to pay them personally. He insisted upon putting stringent provisions prohibiting state debt into the document, and when it was completed he bragged, "I have locked up the treasury and thrown the key away."

Alfred Colquitt was not as well known or as colorful as the other political leaders of the time, although he served as both governor and U.S. senator and was known as one of the "Bourbon Triumvirate" along with Joe Brown and John B. Gordon.

John B. Gordon was the first governor to serve in the new state capitol, taking office in 1887. It would be the first of three terms. He also served two terms as a U.S. senator. But he was even better known as a heroic general during the Civil War.

The son of a preacher, Gordon was precocious and decisive in all he did, beginning with "joining the church" as a preschooler when he was so small he had to stand on a table to give his "confession" before the congregation. That table would end up at the Grace Primitive Baptist Church in Upson County where Artemas was from.

Gordon was a lawyer and a prosperous coalmine manager in Dade County when the war broke out. Totally without any military experience, the twenty-nine-year-old Gordon formed a company of mountaineers called "The Raccoon Roughs." They had no uniforms but all wore coonskin caps. They were mustered in as part of the Sixth Alabama Infantry Regiment, and Gordon was made a lieutenant colonel. He quickly moved up the ranks and was a general by May 1862. He fought in many battles and led one of the daring charges at Gettysburg. At Spotsylvania in 1864, he saved Robert E. Lee's life by stemming a break in the Confederate line and was at Lee's side when the surrender occurred at Appomattox.

Gordon, who sometimes was called "The Praying General," was a pious man all his life. His men literally worshipped him, and one was reported to have said, "Hit would holp a whipped chicken just to look at him fight."

After the war, Gordon wrote his memoirs titled *Reminiscences* and was one of the first public figures to find the lecture circuit profitable. In 1873 he was elected to the U.S. Senate, defeating the popular Alexander H. Stephens, and was reelected in 1879. Then he went on to serve three terms as governor.

Another political leader of note during this period in which Artemas came of age was Thomas E. Watson of Thomson, Georgia. Some have described him as the most charismatic and intellectual politician of his time.

Red-haired and slender, he was "bookish" even at an early age. At fourteen he was writing essays, speeches, prose, and poetry. He went to Mercer for a while but dropped out to teach school and read law. At twenty-one he was admitted to practice law, but his poverty was so acute he could not pay the $10 admission fee to the Bar. The judge instructed the clerk to credit him for the amount.

Within a few years he was one of the three most prosperous trial lawyers in Georgia, the other two being Robert Toombs and Benjamin Harvey Hill. His ability to sway rural juries by speaking the rural idiom made him a legend in his time. Once, while successfully defending a client on the charge of stealing a hog, he pointed to the accuser and said, "I presume from what he says that he could with all ease tell you the sex of a hog, male or female, merely by smelling the gravy."

His travels and courtroom work impressed upon him the low social and political status of farmers, and astutely he saw their need for a champion. His success as a lawyer had made him wealthy, and in 1890 he decided to close his law practice and begin a political career. He ran for Congress and won. His greatest achievement came in 1893 when he passed an amendment to experiment with the free delivery of mail to people living outside the limits of incorporated towns and cities. That was the beginning of what became knows as RFD, Rural Free Delivery, and Watson is credited with being its father. The first official route was in Warren County, Georgia.

He was defeated, however, in 1894, returned to his home, "Hickory Hill" near Thomson, and began the prolific writing period of his life. The books flowed: a two-volume *Story of France*, a biography of Napoleon, novels on all subjects, *Sketches of Roman History, The Life and Times of Andrew Jackson, The Life and Times of Thomas Jefferson*, and many more. He also started magazines, had fiercely loyal supporters around the state and nation, and ran for president several times on the Populist Party ticket.

Yes, Artemas Lester lived in the time of political giants, and these were some of them. He lived when the "New South" was beginning, but it would be a while before much of anything "new" came to the isolated mountains of northeast Georgia. Their ways were still old.

For no American settler anywhere ever put down roots in greater isolation or more total dependence upon himself and his environment than did those Scotch-Irish who were the first settlers. Cut off from the influence of a changing American society outside the ridges, they developed a culture of necessity in which they fashioned their way of life from the rudiments of the Elizabethan heritage they had brought with them. Onto that they grafted a minimal existence based upon what could be found or produced through their own endeavors; that "make-do or do without," as Elder Thomas had called it.

Although sometimes depicted as crude and indolent, most mountain people adhered to a strict code of personal ethics and civility of conduct. They were skilled in the techniques of survival, even if many were academically unlettered. Sensitive to the slurs upon their way of life, they were aggressive and effective, if often unorthodox, in providing for the basic needs of themselves and their loved ones.

Their Spartan diets made them lean and sinewy, and their keen minds made them inquisitive and shrewd. They were experts at hiding their emotions and stoic in enduring the hardships of their primitive society. They were loyal friends who gave unselfishly of themselves to aid those they knew and trusted. They were suspicious of ulterior motives. A stranger or casual visitor could never ascertain their true feelings. But on the other hand, no stranger ever was accorded warmer hospitality than that received by the wayfarer who happened to stop at a mountain cabin. The mountain people were single-minded of purpose, but those who mistook their childlike directness and innate simplicity for slowness were guilty of applying the yardstick of appearances and the values of materialism to a way of life stripped to its most basic fundamentals. It was totally devoid of all the pretensions with which so-called civilized society camouflaged its baser instincts.

Even in the best of times, Appalachian life was hard and barren. Poverty was a general state, but there were no complaints about the absence of luxuries. Medical care was rare, and non-fatal illnesses and injuries were treated with home remedies or simply borne with a fatalistic acceptance of "what must be will be." Families were extended, and three generations often could be found under one roof, the able-bodied caring for both the infirm seniors and the helpless juniors.

It was a patriarchal existence in which the word of the man of the house was law. But it was the woman who generally ran the household and was consulted about family matters. Children had few toys other than rag dolls and "play-purties" they made for themselves. Infant and child mortality was high, and rare was the cabin without an adjacent burial ground populated with tiny graves. Death was an accepted fact of life. "It was his time to go" was the explanation.

The hardest of the hard mountain life was that of the wife or woman of the household. Many were married by the age of fifteen, and nearly all before they were twenty. Large families were the rule, seven to ten children being considered normal and upwards of twenty not being regarded as unusual. Expectant mothers continued their usual work up to several days before the time of birth and were up at their chores again almost as soon as the delivery was over. Most mountain babies were born with the assistance of only a midwife or "granny woman" as she was called.

The old saying about a woman's work never being done probably had its origin in the labors of the mountain woman who not only was a mother to her children, servant to her family, and lover to her husband, but also was the chief field hand and the cook of three hot meals a day. These brave and hardworking women had not yet heard of "the new Georgia."

CHAPTER 8

"A Picture Unsurpassed"

The sun was straight up in a blue sky when Artemas forded Brasstown Creek. *Midday, January 17, 1885,* he noted. The creek was about two feet deep, he figured as he observed slender shelves of ice clinging to the banks. In the shallows he could see that the creek bottom and sand bars were lined with hundreds of beautiful rocks. Washed smooth over thousands of years, they were yellow, amber, brown, and white. Artemas remembered the Cherokee word "Chattahoochee" means "flowering rocks." *They have a way with names,* he thought admiringly.

He looked to his right to the southeast across a wide stretch, maybe five acres of "new ground" that had recently been cleared. He could see a mountain, or was it two different mountains, rising up out of the valley with two rounded peaks? Later he would learn it was called Double Knobs, and he could see why. He also would notice that the distance between the two peaks seemed to change depending upon where one viewed it from the valley floor.

To the south a long range of mountains stretched in a majestic purple panorama. In the middle of the long mountain range he was admiring, one peak stood above all the rest, reaching almost to heaven it seemed. "I will lift up my eyes." Artemas, a flatlander, understood for the first time what the psalmist had meant by "lift up," and he would never forget it. For the rest of his life when he heard the 101st Psalm, he would think of this view that transfixed him on that winter day.

As he took it in, he suddenly remembered reading what Meriwether Lewis had written in his journal: "I behold the Rocky Mountains for the first time. Oh the joy!" Lewis, of course, was part of the famous Lewis and Clark Expedition that President Thomas Jefferson had chosen to explore the vast, unknown land of the Louisiana Purchase. With twenty-one men imbued with "undaunted courage," they discovered what an unbelievable bargain Jefferson had made. Meriwether Lewis had lived in Georgia when he was a boy; "Merne," he had been called. After he exclaimed, "Oh the joy," the explorers still had a few months to go before they saw the Pacific Ocean in November 1805. It had been a journey of two and a half years, compared to Artemas's of less than three weeks. Lewis had been about the same age as Artemas, and when he reached his thirty-first birthday on the way back, he had written in his journal, "I figure I am halfway through the years I have to spend on this earth." Artemas remembered Lewis was sadly wrong; he was dead at thirty-five.

Thinking about it, Artemas could not help being struck with his own mortality and wondered where would he be at that age. Would the goal of his expedition bear fruit? What would he accomplish before he began his journey back over the mountains? Old Beulah plodded along, around a bend, down a short but steep hill, across a small branch, and up another steep hill, and there was the graveyard and church on his right. What had Mr. Butt called it? "Union Cemetery"?

"Union" was a popular name up here in this area, Artemas remembered. He would later learn that in 1832 there was a strong and favorable feeling in the mountain region toward the federal government. After all, that was who was removing the Cherokees. John C. Calhoun's theory of Nullification may have been popular in other places in the South, but in the mountains it threatened disunion. So when the county's first state representative, John Thomas, was asked what should they call the new county, he answered, "Union, for nothing but Union-like men live in it." Later in 1861 when Georgia seceded from the Union, Representative William G. Butt voted against secession. Both Towns County delegates, the Reverends Elijah Kimsey and John Corn, although slave owners, also voted against secession.

When Union County was first created and the land surveyed by James Blair and John Love, it was about 1,000 square miles of land. In 1854 the western side was made into Fannin County. In 1856 the southern tip was given to Gilmer County, and that same year the eastern part, where Artemas now found himself, was taken to form Towns

County. In all, Union County had been cut by about two-thirds to roughly 320 square miles.

It was not the union of Abraham Lincoln; it was the union of Andrew Jackson. "Old Hickory" had once offered a toast: "To our Union; it must be preserved." His vice president John C. Calhoun, a "states-righter," had countered with a toast of his own: "To our Union, *after* our liberty most dear." It was the beginning of trouble in that administration.

Artemas still had not met nor seen another living soul since he left Mr. Butt at the Track Rock Post Office, and there were no structures he could see except the church house on the hill above the graveyard. Then a few hundred yards further he saw a log house, which Artemas figured must be the Bryson cabin Mr. Butt had told him about.

John Bryson had come into Brasstown Valley in the summer of 1835 from Cullowhee, North Carolina. Legend had it that he first traded a rifle to the Indians for 60 acres. A few years later he purchased 160 acres from a Luke White of Lumpkin County. He was thirty-one years old and had been married for eight years to the former Jane Rogers.

At that time there were still Cherokee families living in the valley, each family consisting of seven to ten persons. Three families lived along Brasstown Creek on land that would later be owned by the Dean, Corn, and Nichols families. The heads of the Cherokee families were John Walker, Salagathee, and Yohnuguskee or Drowning Bear. All were full-blood Cherokees, and when Indian agents had come in to make a "valuation of property," the Indians resented it. John Walker's property consisted of a cabin, a smokehouse, a crib, a stable and outhouse, one horse, eighteen peach trees, eight apple trees, and ten acres of land for a value of $205.50. The other two evaluations were much less.

Walker, whose property was the closest to the North

The John Bryson Home

Carolina line, bluntly told the agents that he would not go to Arkansas or take money for his property. The agent quoted him as saying "he wanted to stay where he was." On approaching Drowning Bear, this agent wrote, "This Indian like the last won't show nothing and said he did not understand it." After talking with Drowning Bear, the agent, whether it was John Shaw, George Kellogg, or one of two subordinates named Hutchins and Kelly, then added this accurate observation to his field notes:

> Here is perhaps the most splendidly striking mountain scenery upon the face of the globe. An amphitheater of probably 50 miles in circuit is formed by the Brasstown Mountains encircling a beautiful and fertile valley about 4 miles across interspersed with limpid streams and making upon the whole a picture unsurpassed and rarely if ever equaled for the wildness and grandeur of its scenery.

In this "picture unsurpassed," sixty-two Cherokee households were enumerated, and the average value of these properties was $99.88. Only one hamlet was recorded, Skena, and that contained eight households, including the household of the head man, Toonawah, which was valued at $271.

The Ivy Log area had thirteen Indian farms, and Hemptown Creek had ten. There were others of record along Arkaquah, Bell, and Gum Log creeks. The one with the highest value in the area was a Bell Creek farm evaluated at $307. No cattle were listed by any owner. All acreage was valued at $8.00 an acre, and log cabins at $30.00.

After the Cherokees were removed, the land was carved into 160-acre lots. Levi Polk of Madison County and John Sheffield of Early County were the successful drawers of most of the land in the immediate valley.

John Bryson had built a strong sturdy log home, two rooms 14x16 and 16x18 connected by a breezeway or "dogtrot." He later added an "L" on the back for a dining room and kitchen. The house was much the same when Artemas came by fifty years later. Bryson donated the land for the church and graveyard in 1843, and he and Jane were two of the Old Union Church's charter members. During much of this time, the Bryson cabin served as the post office and John served as postmaster. Beginning in 1842, it was called Brasstown. For three years (1848–1851), it was called Greenwood, then back to Brasstown, and from 1857–1858, it was called Eolia, which then changed to Mount Eolia (1859–1876). John died in 1874, ten years before Artemas came by.

Bryson's two oldest sons were named Tillman and Mangum. The latter lived in the old cabin and was a blacksmith who farmed and served as postmaster of Mt. Eolia until 1876, when it was discontinued and the one at Track Rock where Artemas had stopped was created. His wife was Arminta Jane Corn, known as "Mitty." They had five children. Junious Casinove, or J. C., was the oldest and Artemas got to know him a few months later in July when his two-year-old daughter, Emma, fell into an old abandoned well as she was following a pig. Several hours went by before they could get to her. When they brought her up, she was unconscious and they thought she was dying. Artemas went in to be with the family and watched them as they heated corn and stuck it around her to break the chill. Everyone was relieved when she finally opened her eyes about midnight and uttered "Ma." Artemas, who had led the family in prayer, could not have been happier had she been his own daughter.

Artemas had the names of several families known for giving shelter and food to visiting preachers. One was Mitch Coker, who as "a lad of a boy" living in South Carolina had helped a Lloyd family drive a herd of hogs to Brasstown Valley. They had a daughter named Narcissis to whom Mitch took a liking, so he just stayed and lived with the Lloyds and later married her.

Artemas found the Coker place without much trouble about two miles from where he had crossed Brasstown Creek up on a knoll overlooking beautiful bottom land and the creek to the west. He liked the Cokers at first sight. Four of their children were grown and had moved away. One called "Little Will" had died in childhood a few years before. Two, Felix, about ten, and Mary Lou, about eight, were well-behaved and mannered children. They said little but when asked a question gave short and polite answers. Artemas guessed they were used to having company.

After a hot supper and some talk around the fireplace, Artemas was shown the room where he was to sleep. It had been a long day, and Artemas was ready for bed. He went to sleep quickly that first night in Brasstown Valley. But sometime in the wee hours of the morning, well before daylight, a movement in the small room suddenly awakened Artemas. Half asleep, he thought for a second that someone had crawled under his bed. He let out a cry, and almost immediately Mitch appeared with an oil lamp. They looked around the shadows of the room, searching for an intruder. Under the bed they found it—in a box of quilt scraps was a large mother cat and four meowing newborn kittens.

Artemas would stay with the Cokers off and on for nearly six months and learn a lot from them about the valley, its history, and its people. He also got to know a lot about chickens. Both Mitch and Narcissis enjoyed raising and caring for them. And they were everywhere. They pecked around in the yard, scratched under the front porch, and roosted in the trees. They chased flying bugs in the air or each other if one had a juicy worm in its bill. There were Rhode Island Reds, Plymouth Rocks, and little bantams. There were also "dominickers," a black and white speckled breed. And there was an old rooster with long, thick spurs that was cock of the walk. He would wake you in the morning crowing up the sun, strut and preen and chase hens during the day, and flog little kids.

Artemas learned that "settin' hens" were ornery cusses also. Usually they would make a nest in a special secluded spot in the weeds and honeysuckle, and you couldn't find them. They'd only get off their nest once a day to eat. In three weeks, the little biddies hatched and the hen and her litter were moved to a tee-pee shaped, wooden slats chicken coop with the mother hen inside and the little chicks running in and out underneath the coop. Once Artemas picked up one of her chicks and the mother hen had a fit.

Sometimes the hens and her biddies would have the run of the yard, and it was common to see a hardworking mother hen with her fluffy little yellow—or sometimes black—chicks following along after her. She'd scratch and they would scamper around in the fresh dirt hunting things to eat. If danger in the form of a cat or a snake approached, she'd squat low on the ground with wings outspread, and all the chicks would get safely beneath her. If a little chick got too close to water or strayed too far away, she'd cluck and run frantically back and forth. Artemas figured this was the origin of the expression "she hovers over him like a mother hen."

By the time the chicks were eight to ten weeks old, they could forage for their own food and break away from their mother. When they were "frying size," the males or cocks were separated from the females or pullets. Many of the pullets were kept for laying, and the cocks were sold.

At the Cokers', as in most mountain homes, chicken was a delicacy reserved for Sunday dinner. Mr. Coker would kill the chicken by placing its head on the chopping block at the woodpile with one hand and using one swift stroke from an axe, but Mrs. Coker would take a chicken by its head and with several swift clockwise revolutions of her strong right arm literally would wring the chicken's head right off. She'd be left holding a lifeless head in her hand, and the headless chicken would flop around on the ground for a few minutes slinging blood everywhere until it died. Then she'd dip the chicken in a pot of boiling hot water and begin to pull its feathers off by the handful. After the bird had been totally picked, she would hold the chicken over a fire to singe off all the little pinfeathers Then out would come the entrails. The "craw" was always cut open to see what it had been eating since, of course, a chicken has no teeth. There was an old mountain saying: "scarce as hen's teeth."

The digestive system of a chicken Artemas found fascinating. When the chicken swallows grains of corn, the food goes down its gullet to a pouch called a crop or "craw" and is moistened there. From the crop it passes to the glandular part of the stomach where it is mixed with certain gastric juices. The food is then passed into the gizzard, a purplish, muscular part of the stomach lined with a thick membrane. In the gizzard the food is crushed by the movements of the muscular walls and stones and gravel that have been swallowed by the chicken. The gizzard along with the tough neck were always the last pieces left on the platter.

The breast was cut to have a wishbone, or "pully bone," and youngsters had a lot of fun pulling the v-shaped bone. The one who got the longest piece had his wish come true.

Mr. Coker considered white eggs inferior. "You crack them in a frying pan and the white is thin and runny. The yolk usually slides over to one side. With a brown egg, the white is thicker and the yolk stands up in the middle where it's supposed to. You see, Artemas, chickens with red ear lobes lay brown eggs. Chickens with white ear lobes lay white eggs. Look closely. The ear lobe is slightly behind and under the chicken's eye and right back of the wattles, the pink or red flesh that dangles beneath the bill. You can make the comb and wattles redder by feeding the chickens cracked red pepper in their feed. In addition to helping their complexion, the pepper makes them lay better."

"Chickens only lay for about two years," Mr. Coker explained. "When one can place three fingers together flat against the hen's rear area and feel the bones that far apart, the hen is through as a layer and might as well be put in the soup pot."

Elder Thomas had also given Artemas the name of Bill Dean as one to look up when he got to the valley. Dean had come from the Mossy Creek area of White County. Mitch knew where he lived and gave Artemas directions to his place situated on the crest of a hill overlooking a fertile valley to the west with Brasstown Creek running through it. Several acres had been cleared, and a narrow

The Bill Dean Home

rutted road had been carved through it. Artemas later learned the road went to Murphy, North Carolina, about twenty miles away. The state line was less than five miles down Brasstown Creek, which emptied into the Hiawassee River a few miles further to the west. To the north, Wagon Road Gap could be seen. And beyond that, Artemas was told, was Woodgrove, a little settlement at the foot of the mountain made up mostly of the Wood and Groves families. Then a few miles to the east was the county seat, Hiawassee.

Hiawassee, first spelled "Hiwassee," had been incorporated October 24, 1870, fourteen years after Towns County had been formed and the town laid out. Like so many places in the mountains, the name was derived from the Cherokee word *a-yu-wa-si,* meaning either "meadow," "savanna," or "pretty fawn." It was said to be the name of a Cherokee Indian princess who had an ill-fated love affair with a warrior from the Catawba tribe named "Nottley" or "Daring Horseman." Legend had it that Hiawassee's father objected to a marriage and told Nottley he could marry his daughter only if he found where the waters from the east side of the mountains united with the waters from the west side of the mountains. The chief thought it was an impossible achievement. But Nottley searched and searched, and one day when he was about to give up, while resting and thinking of his love of Hiawassee, he saw three small fawns move toward a lake. To his great surprise, there were two streams flowing into it, one from the east and the other from the west. He was overjoyed, but still the chief would not give permission, so the two lovers leaped to their deaths together off a high rock mountain cliff, probably Mount Yonah in White County, which was named for a great bear that inhabited that area. A similar legend has the lovers named Sautee and Nacoochee.

Bill Dean, like Mr. Butt, was a talkative, friendly fellow. "Pshaw yes, Bud Miller, Andy Allen, Billy Sargent, and I came over those mountains together from Mossy Creek. Magnum and Mitty let me live with them when I first got here. But Bud stopped in Choestoe, had that chance to be a teacher. He'd do it free, you know? And Billy, he's got blacksmithing in his blood just like Bud's got teaching in his. Billy is going to make more money though. You know what he charges to shoe a horse? Seventy-five damn cents. 'Scuse me preacher. And besides that he pulls teeth. Me, I'm going to raise me some lawyers. 'Course, I ain't married yet, but I've got my eye on Kittie Bryson. Yessir, I want some lawyers in the family. I'm tired of making out these deeds for everybody that comes along that ain't got no money. I'll have a store going up right away. The mercantile business is going to be good. I told Bud Miller that, but all he wants to do is teach, read the Bible, and quote folks you never heard of. His wife died recently; she was from Mossy Creek too."

The man wouldn't stop talking, so Artemas just listened. Bill Dean was about thirty years old, maybe still in his twenties and with all those big ideas. He later learned that Dean's father also had been a Methodist circuit rider, Reverend James M. Dean, but Bill Dean had never mentioned it. That was in his past, Artemas thought; Bill was thinking of his future.

"I'm going to build me a big house here; this is some of the old John Bryson property, and I ain't going to be long in doing it. These two rooms you see now are going to become ten rooms before I'm through. 'Course you won't see it. Them Methodists will have you in Waycross at the other end of the state before they're through with you. I've got property up in the Kirby Cove, a hundred acres at least, and more down on Gum Log. I've already got a store down there and had a house there before I sold it to come here. I'm going to use some of that money to buy me one of them 'cap and ball' rifles. Better than the old flint lock, I hear."

Artemas realized he would have to interrupt this man if he were going to get a word in edgewise. "I want to start a school here, an institute," he blurted out.

That stopped Dean cold. He cocked his head to one side and, unlike him, managed only one word: "What?"

"An institute for these mountain youth. Where can they go right now to get an education? Miles away, and their families can't afford that." Artemas crowded all his pent-up thoughts into the conversation before Dean could regain his composure.

But Dean wasn't speechless for long. "An 'in-sti-tute,'" he said, drawing it out sarcastically. "You just came through town if you can call it that." Then Dean grew serious. "You'll be doing good to round up a dozen students. Where's this school gonna be? Where you going to get the teachers? Who's going to pay them? My daddy was a circuit rider," he finally disclosed. "He preached sermons, he saved souls, he buried people and married people." Dean was once again his talkative self. "Did the Bishop know you had this damn fool idea when he assigned you to come up here?"

"Now he does," Artemas said. "I wrote him after I got the assignment. I want to call it McTyeire Institute in his honor. He's just written a book on the history of Methodism. Ten years ago, Bishop Holland McTyeire got Cornelius Vanderbilt to put up the money for that big university in Nashville, and he started the *Nashville Christian Advocate*. I'd say he deserves it."

"Well, that might get you ten dollars from the Conference," Dean replied cynically. "Look, I've been bragging about this place. I think it's got a future. And they also do over the mountain in Hayesville, North Carolina, for that matter. John Hicks has already got a school over there. This valley is some of God's most beautiful work, but it ain't Choestoe. They value learning over there."

For the first time, Artemas interrupted, "They'd send their children here if we had an institution to further their education." He had not planned on having this conversation on his second day in the valley, but here he was arguing with one of its leading citizens whom he had thought would be favorable.

"Where you going to put it?" Dean, ever the pragmatist, asked.

"I don't know, we'll have to find a place," Artemas answered.

"*We* hell," Dean shot back. "You mean *you'll* have to find a place. 'Scuse me, preacher; you've just taken me by surprise. I'll think about it. Are you right sure the Bishop is for this?"

"He believes more in education than anyone I know," Artemas answered honestly. "He helped start one of the biggest up in Nashville. That's why I want to call it McTyeire Institute."

"There's not enough children in this valley, not enough in this county or even surrounding ones. We're isolated up here." Dean continued to argue, now gently as with a child. "Spend the night with me tomorrow night and let me think about it more."

When Artemas told the Cokers that night about his dream and the conversation with Dean, Mrs. Coker's first words were "He's a talker."

Mitch added, "Yes, and a doer. It is quite a dream though, Artemas," he said, almost in the same tone as Dean's. "There's less than a dozen families in this valley."

Artemas constantly had to remind himself that his first duty was to serve the churches in the area to which he had been assigned. He found he had two Zions. One was called "Zion-across-the-line" and was near the Track Rock Post Office not far from a small branch called Bitter Creek. The other was "Zion-on-the-river," several miles east of Hiawassee on the Wyly Road or Unicoi Turnpike. It had an interesting history for both the Methodists and Baptists. Each had a church within one hundred yards of the other at the site on Hiawassee River. Sometimes the sounds of their singing would overlap. It was said that the beautiful Towns County River Valley where it was located had been traded from the Indians for three pieces of gingerbread. Another church was in Hiawassee, a town that had a tippling house for twenty-five years before it had a church, but then it became a church community dominated by the Baptist stalwarts, the McConnell family. A Baptist church had just been established there a few years before in 1882. The pastors were the Reverend Elijah Kimsey and Elisha Hedden with W. L. Sutton as clerk. The town had given the property for the church when the county was laid out. The Methodists and Presbyterians were also given sites, but the latter never used their property.

After the Civil War, William Ross McConnell moved from North Carolina and settled in the Bell Creek area. Later he moved into Hiawassee and built a brick home on the hill near the Baptist church that would later be built. One of his eight children was Fernando C. McConnell, who married Emma England. He was known as "Ferd," and at the time Artemas was in the county, he had just finished at the Southern Baptist Theological Seminary in Louisville, Kentucky, and was taking advanced work at Mercer University. Big things would be in store for this gifted young man. His initials "F.C.," it would be said, stood for "forensic cyclone."

CHAPTER 9

The Funeral

Artemas had been in Brasstown Valley only two weeks when he had his first funeral. When he heard that the matriarch of the Bryson family, Jane Rogers Bryson, had died after being bedridden for six years, he went immediately to pay his respects and see what he could do. When he arrived a large crowd had already gathered at the fifty-year-old log cabin. Some were standing on the porch and others had spread out into the yard. Which ones were family and which ones were neighbors Artemas did not know; there were so many.

Suddenly, Jane's son Mangum Bryson came through the door and greeted him. "Thanks for coming, preacher; we knew it was coming but it's still hard to take. Come in and let's have a prayer."

Artemas ducked through the door and saw the corpse lying on what was called "the cooling board," three planks across two sawhorses. Mrs. Bryson had died while sitting up in bed, and they wanted to get the body straightened out before the "stiffening," or "cold death" as some called it, set in. Artemas understood that and instantly remembered his mother had once told a story about a corpse suddenly sitting up in the coffin. It scared everyone, and then someone explained it was the same position he had died in. So he understood why the body was tied to the board. They also had already pushed the eyelids down and weighted them with a penny on each one. The coins would often remain right up to the time of the funeral and be buried with the deceased. They also had placed a saucer of salt on the stomach, which some believed would dehydrate the body and keep it from swelling. The hair was already neatly combed. Obviously someone had taken charge, and it was obvious from the way everyone deferred to her that it was Mangum's wife, "Mitty," a woman with dark hair parted in the middle and tightly pulled into a neat bun in the back.

Hardly looking up, she said to no one in particular, "Get out her best dress." As her daughter Kitty scampered off to get it, she added, "Let's start working on the lining of the casket."

Mountaineers were known for their preplanning, and Mr. Bryson had years before built his wife's casket out of walnut, explaining matter-of-factly, "Pine will rot in a year." When Mangum mentioned what he had said, it set off a discussion among a few of the men folk about what wood made the best casket. As they talked, Artemas looked around the room. He saw that a sheet had been hung over a mirror above a table, and Mangum, noticing him, whispered that many believed another death would quickly occur if the mirror in the room was not covered. Some of the women hovered around talking, and two sat on the edge of the bed. Mitty Bryson was not among them; she was too busy deciding which quilt would make the best padding for the coffin. When she found the appropriate one, she headed out the door and started walking toward the barn where the casket was kept. Artemas noticed that Kitty, her teenaged daughter, quickly joined her. They talked for a few minutes, and then Kitty returned to the house obviously with an assignment of her mother's to fulfill.

"We've got to start digging the grave as soon as we can. Any volunteers? You know where the plot is," Kitty told the group. Six men immediately left the yard and porch and started walking toward the graveyard, which was less than a half-mile away. Two went in another direction to round up more gravediggers and get shovels and mattocks. "Bring a pick if you've got one. That ground is might rocky," Artemas heard one say. "And get an axe for them roots," he added. There would be more than enough helpers to do the necessary work. It was a communal duty and a family duty and they would respond in droves. They would work in shifts of four, and they would make sure the foot of the grave was toward the east and the head toward the west. Placing the face toward the rising sun was important because many believed that the rising sun was symbolic of the Resurrection and that when Christ returned on Judgment Day He would come from the east and the dead would then rise and participate in the Second Coming.

As the day wore on, kinfolks, friends, and neighbors all came by the Bryson home to pay their respects to one of the valley's oldest and best-known citizens. More food than could be eaten by an army filled the tables and every flat place in the house. The furniture had all been moved to the side or out into the dog trot so there would be room around the corpse. Frequently, Mitty would wipe the face of Mrs. Bryson with a cloth soaked in vinegar.

Artemas heard Mangum explain to someone that his mama had felt better that morning and had wanted to sit up in bed. She had talked for a while and then grew silent, and they thought she was asleep. When Mitty went closer to take a look, Mrs. Bryson said softly, "I am going." Quickly Mitty realized she had died and went running to the field to tell the men who were working there.

Arminta Jane Bryson, called "Mitty," was the daughter of the Reverend Alfred Corn. The Corns, like the Brysons, were among the first of the pioneer families in Brasstown Valley. Reverend Corn had done mission work with the Cherokees before their removal, served as pastor at Old Union Baptist for twenty years, and later would help organize West Union Baptist Church. He would conduct the funeral service and, much to the surprise of Artemas, had asked the new Methodist preacher to help him. Artemas felt accepted and honored, and the more he saw of Pastor Corn the more he would come to respect the man. He had a grandson whom he had raised named John Alfred Corn who would become one of the most respected persons in the area, a large landowner, stock raiser, and political leader, eventually serving several terms as a state representative and senator.

By midnight, Artemas realized that he had better give thought to what he would say at the funeral service the next day. He sat in a corner of the room and prayed for some appropriate words. He had already learned that the service should last at least two hours, and longer would be acceptable. Thinking and praying, he dozed off and didn't wake until daylight when Mitty, who must have been up all night, offered him a cup of coffee. He thanked her, quickly drank it down, and went outside where there were still about a dozen men sitting on the edge of the porch or leaning against the posts.

Artemas noticed that Mangum and his brother Tilmon stood apart from the rest of the crowd. "Two grieving sons," he said to a man next to him.

"And a grandson," the man quickly responded and introduced himself as J. C., Mangum's boy. "We're all kin," he said as he looked around the porch. Artemas did not know it at the time, but Mangum had joined the Confederate Army when the war began and then, sometime later after seeing the mistreatment of one of his uncles by some bushwhackers, joined the Union Forces. Tilmon, who had been a lieutenant in the Georgia Militia before the war, followed his brother. Most of the Bryson grandchildren were grown. One of Tilmon's, named for her grandmother, was called "Little Mitty."

Artemas said goodbye to the mourners, who had stayed up all night, and began his walk back to the Cokers'. Along the way he continued to think of the service and what he should say. When he arrived, the Cokers were finishing breakfast and offered him some eggs, side meat, and biscuits. Although he had eaten some of the feast at the wake, he found he was starved to death and ate heartily. He then went to his room and put on another shirt, wiped his boots clean, and set off back to the church for the two o'clock service. He got there in plenty of time to take a look at the gravesite and talk to some of the crowd that was already beginning to gather. About an hour before time for the service to begin, the casket arrived on a wagon drawn by two big mules. The six men who, because of their closeness to the deceased, had been selected as pallbearers then carried the casket on their shoulders, since there were no handles, into the church and placed it in front of the pulpit on two sawhorses that had been draped in black cloth. Suddenly, Mitty appeared out of nowhere and checked to see if the men had opened the casket to make sure the corpse was still straight after the bumpy ride and ready for public viewing. Artemas could see that she also carried an arrangement of some evergreen leaves he had never seen before. As if reading his mind, she explained that they were "galax" she was planning to put on the grave. Artemas knew that the word "cemetery" came from a Greek word meaning "sleeping place," and he hoped that Mrs. Bryson would be satisfied with the service and sleep well beside her beloved husband, John.

On his walk to the church Artemas continually had sent up prayers that he could meet the challenge: not only being young, but being a Methodist in a Baptist church and a stranger to all but a few of these mountain people.

Men and women, some in their Sunday best and some in their everyday work clothes, kept up a steady stream of entering the church, walking to the front and standing for awhile to view the body, and then finding a seat in the rear. Almost half the church had been set aside for the family. *Surely there aren't that many Brysons and Corns,* Artemas thought to himself. But there were, and more. They filled one entire side of the church, and some of the earlier arrivals got up and stood in the back as they gave their seats to family members.

The song leader, a heavy-set man with a thick neck and coal black hair and beard, started off with an old Fanny Crosby hymn:

Rescue the perishing, care for the dying
Snatch them in pity from sin and the grave
Tell men of Jesus, the mighty to save
Rescue the perishing, care for the dying
Jesus is merciful, Jesus will save.

They sang all four verses. Sometimes the song leader would recite the words of a line and the congregation would follow in song. Artemas liked the way he bore down on that line in the third verse: "Chords that are broken will unbreak once more." He was watching young Kitty and thought he detected some relief in her face.

Next came "Love Divine, All Love Excelling" and it pleased Artemas that the words of the great Charles Wesley were being sung in Old Union Baptist Church.

Reverend Corn then got up and gave some of the facts of life of the deceased, pointing out that she had come to the valley with her husband more than fifty years before. He talked of John's woodworking skill and cabinet making and said, "Just look at the casket, solid walnut. There won't be another one like it on this hillside." He paused to take a deep breath and added, "Ever."

Now it was Artemas's turn. He explained that he was a newcomer, a Methodist from middle Georgia who had not known Mrs. Bryson very long. "But it is obvious," he said looking at the crowded left side of the church, "that she came from good stock. Let us pray."

He led them in prayer. "When death comes, many are crushed; the way can look dark and the road steep and the load heavy." He prayed longer than he had intended, but the Spirit seemed to move him. He was talking to God on behalf of the grieving family, and when he ended with his "amen," a louder "amen" came from both sides of the packed church.

Now Reverend Corn returned to speak of his daughter's mother-in-law and the matriarch of the large Bryson family. First, he mentioned what many knew, that she and her husband had donated the land for the cemetery where she was about to be buried. He then turned to the passages he had marked in his well-worn Bible. He first recited the 23rd Psalm. *What could ever be more appropriate at a funeral?* Artemas thought as he listened to those familiar words: "The Lord is my shepherd, I shall not want . . ." and then "Yea though I walk through the valley of the shadow of death, I will fear no evil, for Thou are with me . . . ." He ended, "Surely goodness and mercy shall follow me all the days of my life, and I will dwell in the house of the Lord forever."

He then turned to the words of Jesus found in John 3:16: "For God so loved the world that he gave his only begotten Son that whosoever believeth in him shall not perish but have everlasting life." And John 14:24: "In my Father's house are many mansions; if it were not so, I would have told you. I go to prepare a place for you, and I will come again and receive you unto myself, that where I am you may be also. And whither I go ye know, and the way ye know."

It was a wonderful, tender message, and too soon it was time for Artemas to speak. He tried to tell the mourners that those of us who are Christians know that death is not the end of existence any more than birth is the beginning of life. That as a baby she had been alive before she even saw the light of day. That baby came into one new world upon her birth, just like now Mrs. Bryson had gone into another new world upon her death.

He told the story of when John Quincy Adams was eighty years old and a friend had inquired, "How is John Quincy Adams today?" The former president responded, "John Quincy Adams is fine thank you but this old house in which he lives is becoming dilapidated, in fact, almost inhabitable, and I think John Quincy Adams will have to move out before long. But he himself is well, quite well." Artemas talked about grief and how it is natural to cry. "But beyond the vale of tears, there is life above." He talked about how Paul had taught that the sufferings of the present time do not compare to the glory that will be revealed in another time. He explained the best he could again that life on earth was just one part of our existence. Artemas was caught up in the moment; God was giving him the words as he had prayed He would.

He wanted them to know that the deceased was not really dead, "just gone." He told them, "In our Father's house above she is waiting on us and we will soon join her." That brought Artemas to the lesson of the resurrection: "Because I live, you will live also. He who believes in the Son of God has eternal life." He must have preached an hour; he could feel his shirt was soaked through as he finally led them in prayer, praying for a woman he hardly knew but all in the congregation did. "Not one of us will ever forget her. We will continue to receive a blessing from having known her." He invoked the Lord, "You are the One who gives us hope and light and joy." He ended by thanking God "for the victory, eternal life through Jesus Christ, our crucified, risen, and loving Lord."

Although Artemas had been to many funerals and conducted several in Lincolnton, this was his first one in the mountains. After "Amazing Grace," there was then another viewing of the body in the casket. Silently, row by row came by until the immediate family was last. There was crying, audible sighs, and a few of the grown children lay across the casket for several minutes or knelt on the floor beside it. While this was going on, the other members of the congregation remained in silent respect, some of them crying, hugging one another, and blowing their noses.

After much time had passed, the lid of the coffin was placed on top but not securely fastened. There would be one more viewing at the gravesite itself, Artemas was to learn. It was about 100 yards to the gravesite from the church, and it was rough walking. A mule pulled a sled with the casket on it while two teenage grandchildren rode along to make sure the lid of the coffin did not fall off.

The pallbearers were responsible for getting the casket in the ground but not until one last viewing by the family. Then the casket was placed over the open grave on two planks. Two ropes were placed under the coffin at each end and the planks removed. Slowly the four men, two on each side, lowered it until it reached the bottom of the grave. Then the planks were placed above the casket and the dirt was filled in. Before that, Reverend Corn said a short prayer and quoted the verses in Ecclesiastes and Genesis: "Then the dead will return to the earth as it was and the spirit will return to God who gave it. For you are dust and to dust you shall return." The family remained until the grave was filled and then went back to the home where neighbors had prepared even more food.

Artemas stayed until the family was leaving. Mitty, accompanied by Kitty, thanked him for officiating and said goodbye. He walked back to the Coker family place with two of the men who had waited on him. He ate a corndodger with some buttermilk and went to bed.

The day after the funeral, Artemas went to see Bill Dean. He found Bill at his home working on the door. He had it removed from its hinges and was busy chipping away at its bottom. Deep in thought, he barely looked up when Artemas arrived and grunted a sign of recognition. A few minutes later when he had finished what he was doing, he looked up as if he had just discovered Artemas was present and gave a cordial "How are you?"

Artemas had been waiting for that greeting. He had slept fitfully all night worried how his first funeral in the valley had gone. "How did I do?" he blurted out.

His new friend gave him a slow penetrating look as if to say, "Do you really want to know?" After the pause he looked at the young preacher and slowly answered, "Well, what you did was good, very good, in fact." He paused and continued, "It's what you didn't do."

Somewhat taken aback at the mountain man's directness, Artemas managed to ask, "What do you mean?"

Artemas was about to learn what every man, woman, and child in the valley knew all too well. Don't ask Bill Dean his opinion on anything unless you really want to hear it.

"Well, to begin with, a funeral message is for two sets of people who are always there. One group is the family. They should be comforted. They want to know their loved one is going to be with God and that someday, if they live good lives, they will see them again. You handled that as good as I've heard, especially not even knowing the deceased. But you didn't even acknowledge that other group."

Artemas couldn't help interrupting, "Who are they? Who are you talking about?"

"I'll tell you who." Bill, the son of an old preacher, couldn't wait to answer. "Every person in that church, no matter what age, was thinking someday I'll be up there in that coffin and what's going to happen to me? Will it be heaven or hell for me? Will I be ready to go? That's your second group. You could have saved some souls. You could have carried them straight to Jesus. In my store I can tell when a man is ready to buy. Can't you tell when someone is ready to buy? Don't you know when there's a sale to be made? John Wesley made thousands of them in his day. Couldn't you feel the emotion? The time was ripe for some hellfire. I hate to say it, but you've got to scare some people into repentance. You had a captive audience and you didn't take advantage of it. Make'm see hell if they don't mend their ways and make'm see heaven if they do. A funeral ain't just about the dead, Artemas, it's about the living, and don't ever forget it." He turned back to working on the door.

Artemas would preach many funerals during the remaining years of his ministry, and he would never forget Bill Dean's lesson that day.

CHAPTER 10

The Teacher

School was not in session when Artemas first came through Choestoe, so he returned to spend a week in late July. Schools at that time opened around July 15 after the corn had been "laid by" or had its final hoeing before it began to silk and tassel. About the first of September, there would be a break of two weeks when the students would be needed to help pull fodder. When the Reverend Hamby had learned that Artemas wanted to see the best school in Union County and meet its teacher, the first name he gave him was William Jasper "Bud" Miller who had been hired in 1880 expressly for the purpose of teaching at Hood's Chapel in Upper Choestoe. When Enoch Shuler hired him, his brief but specific instructions were, "You are the school teacher. Put the rod on the boys if they need it, and hold up morality in Hood Community. Learn the children to be polite and kind. And learn them to respect their parents and God. And learn them to be patriotic, too. It is not enough for them to be perfect in their lessons. They must learn to live good lives and hold up our government."

A few years later Miller, whose wife, Florence Edmundsin, had died and left him with six children to raise, had moved to another school that he called Auburn. Schools were being created and discontinued as the school-age populations fluctuated. At this time, in the Choestoe Valley alone there were Liberty, Tan Yard, Hood's Chapel, and Coon Run Hollow. There was also Wild Boar Institute, located, it was said, "under Blood Mountain and founded by Tom Henson." The schools met in "meeting houses" or in private homes; the schools did not own the building. Auburn was the largest in Choestoe with about thirty-five students. Each school had one teacher and each teacher taught primarily from the same text, *The Elementary Spelling Book by Noah Webster*, more commonly known as *The Blue Book Speller*.

W. J. (Bud) Miller and wife Jane

Bud had brought several other books with him from White County that he used at different times and for different students depending upon their age and rate of advancement. One was *Sanford's Intermediate Arithmetic* and another *Sanford's High Analytical Arithmetic*. Bud was a fanatic, some said, on children learning their multiplication tables.

When a boy would enter the school he would remove his hat, and when a girl entered the doorway she would always curtsy. Some schools had two doors, one for the boys to enter and one for the girls.

The schools would close late in October, so, of course, the teachers had to have other occupations. Some were also preachers. Bud started a store not long after he arrived, and along with being a teacher and a merchant he also farmed. He also became superintendent of the Salem Methodist Sunday Schools and would hold that position for thirty-five years.

In those days, the schools had no paper, pencils, or blackboards. Much was done by recitation, and often more than one student would be reciting at a time. Some called them "blab" schools because of this. Abraham Lincoln once said he went to a "blab" school for a while. They did use slates and slate pencils. The students sat on the benches with the slates resting on their knees, using them for arithmetic problems almost exclusively. To erase their writing, students would spit on the slates and then wipe them clean with the heel of a hand or the bottom of a closed fist.

Some children brought their lunch in a "poke" or paper sack that would be carefully folded and used time and time again. Water came from a nearby spring, and a dipper, usually a common long-handle gourd, was used by all.

Bud had a style and range of information that Artemas found amazing. It was student participation carried to the maximum. Bud would sometimes jump from subject to subject from student to student. "Vesco, what is nine times nine? Harve, what's the verb in this sentence? Lannie, what is the second of the Ten Commandments? Anyone, how do you spell 'geography'?" He would help them along. "Remember," he would say, "George Elliot's old granny ran a pig home yesterday. G-E-O-G-R-A-P-H-Y, geography." There were first-year students and there were students who had been there since Bud came three years before. When a student would give the right answer to a tough question, Bud's favorite response was, "Boy, oh boy!" in sincere admiration. Sometimes he would preface his remarks with "Hear this," which meant something important and worth remembering was about to be said. Smiling to himself, Artemas compared it to "verily," which Jesus sometimes used before he said something profound. Unlike some teachers, Bud was not afraid to say "I don't know" or "I'll find out" when a student posed a difficult question. He was not like that teacher in another school who, when asked what the subjunctive mode was, answered, "The subjunctive mode denotes doubt. That means no one is supposed to understand it."

Bud once stopped abruptly and announced, "Take what you want, saith the Lord, take it and pay for it. That's not in the Bible, well, not exactly, but it should be. You can have anything you want in this country, but it has a cost. You want to go to college? Study! You want to learn to play the fiddle? Practice! Every reward has a cost. Even having a good corn crop. Freedom is not free. We have to pay for it." Another time he told the students, "You can beat half the people just by working hard and another forty percent by standing for something. Do them both and you're part of that special ten percent."

Another gem that Artemas heard him use was "The man who takes no interest in politics is not careless. He is useless."

Bud knew all the children's parents and sometimes would bring them into the class discussion. "Ask your father about that," or "I wonder what your mother would have to say." Artemas was as mesmerized as the children by Bud's wide-ranging discussions and lectures. You couldn't really call them lectures because the inevitable questions would come rapid fire every few minutes.

Obviously, Bud wanted the students to understand they were on this earth for a limited amount of time and they had to make the most of it. Learning was not sissy; it could be enjoyable and even profitable. Once, out of the clear blue sky, he announced, "Thucydides said in his funeral oration of Pericles, 'We cherish wisdom without efficiency.' What does this mean? Anybody?" This schoolmaster believed that persistence could overcome anything and wanted each of his students to understand that.

"You know how you learned to walk?" he would ask. Blank stares would be the answer. "When you first tried to walk you fell down. But you didn't stay down; you got back up and tried again. That's how you accomplish anything worthwhile in life. When things go wrong as they sometimes will, don't quit. Get up and try again."

Every few days he would remind them, "'Can't' is the worst word ever written or spoken. Do not use it."

Bud would use riddles to get student participation and "whit their wit," as he called it. One was "The more you feed it the more it will grow high. But if you give it water, it will surely die." A fire. "What is it that goes all over the house in the day and stands in the corner at night?" A broom. After a bunch of commotion that taxed Bud's power of discipline, the students finally got the correct answer. They failed on the third riddle, as did Artemas. "What walks on four legs in the morning, two at noon, and three at night?" It was a riddle that the Greeks had used hundreds of years before. "Man" is the answer. "A baby crawls on all fours, a man in the noontime of his life stands upright on two feet, and then as an old man he walks with a cane."

No one was left out. In the middle of the arithmetic lesson, he would suddenly and solemnly declare, "And now abideth faith, hope, charity, these three; but the greatest of these is what? Class?" A resounding "charity" came from every one of the students.

Bud not only taught the Bible; he used Aesop's fables often. In the week Artemas was there, he heard "The Tortoise and the Hare," "The Bundle of Sticks," and "The Boy who Cried Wolf." Everyday happenings at home or in life were then applied to each. Once when a boy earnestly tried but answered a question incorrectly, Bud gave this encouragement: "That's all right. If you can't be the bell cow, lope up in the herd."

Bud had named the school "Auburn" to the bewilderment of all. "It's from Goldsmith's 'Deserted Village,'" he tried to explain to some of the frontiersmen who thought this well-read man was a little "off." "Sweet Auburn, loveliest village of the plain," he would recite, as if that should be reason enough. If there were still a puzzled look on the parent's face, he would continue, "Ill fares the land, to hastening ills a prey, where wealth accumulates, and men decay."

More than one hard-working man who had no material possessions to speak of would walk away shaking his head and saying, "There ain't much wealth accumulating around here. What's Bud talking about?" Secretly, Artemas thought, *Bud sees himself as the schoolmaster described in Goldsmith's poem: "And still they gazed and wonder grew, how one small head could hold all he knew."*

Bud loved Shakespeare and quoted him second only to the Bible. His favorite was the fatherly advice Polonius gave his son Laertes, Hamlet's friend, when he was going off to get an education: "To thine own self be true, and it follows as the day the night, thou cannot be false with any man."

Once, Artemas heard him recite Hamlet's "To Be or Not to Be" speech and then quickly ask the students, "What's one's 'mortal coil,' can anyone tell me?"

Another favorite verse he had the older students memorize was from *King Richard II*: "My honor is my life, both grow in one. Take honor from me, and my life is done."

Another favorite question was to ask a student, "What is it that makes your heart 'leap up'?" Bud thought the answer told a lot about a youth and that it was sad when one could not name a single thing that made his heart leap up.

Discipline was good in Bud Miller's school, for he usually taught with a large switch in his hand. The Reverend Hamby had told Artemas the story of one father coming to the school and calling Bud outside. It seems he was mad that his son had been whipped the day before. When Bud got outside, the parent quickly told him, "You whipped my boy yesterday and I'm going to whip you."

Bud answered, "Are you right sure you can do it?"

"Hell, yes, you're nothing but a stinking coward."

The teacher quietly answered, "Well, I never posed as a brave man. If I were up against any kind of danger, I suppose I'd be afraid."

"You're up against it right now, you confounded fool," the angry parent exploded, as he hauled off and hit Bud right on the nose. Now bloody but unbowed, Bud returned the blow with one of his own. As some of the children looked on out the partially opened door, Bud let the blustering parent have it with a right upper cut to the chin. The man hit the ground with a thud. The fight was over. But the disagreement wasn't. The teacher was taken to court with the parent charging the teacher with "intent to murder." The local justice of the peace held the trial, and the case was quickly dismissed.

"I appeal," cried the parent, "I'm going to take this to the Big Court in Blairsville."

"Go ahead," said the squire, "but that judge will give you the same advice I am."

"What's that advice?" the man demanded.

The justice of the peace answered, "Never pick a fight with anyone unless you are sure you can finish it." And then the squire turned to Bud. "and I've got some advice to say to you."

"Yes, sir, Squire, what is it?" Bud asked, now frightened himself.

The answer came quickly. "Next time a bully picks a fight with you, hit him with your left hand and save that right for some balking, ornery, corn-fed mule. Court's adjourned," he bellowed, as he spit a stream of tobacco juice in the spittoon at his feet.

One of the biggest days in Choestoe—especially in the lives of the youth—was "Children's Day" at Salem Methodist Church. It was one of Bud's greatest teaching experiences, and he gloried in it.

It was held on a special Sunday in June and was a combination of singing, speaking, reciting, acting, reading poems, pantomimes, debating, and what was called "the rose drill." It was held on a platform built beneath the trees at the church. Some called it a "brush arbor."

"Bud is big on elocution," someone always said, and then someone else would respond, "The training one gets from Children's Day will stick with them for the rest of their life." "I wish we'd had them in our day," another would add. "And Bud's big on being on time. He tells those children that when they are late it's as same as telling the other person your time is more important than their time. He's like 'Cussin' Tom' Henson, you know, he says that if you have an engagement with a dog and if one of you has to be late, let it be the dog."

The poem most recited on Children's Day was Alfred Lord Tennyson's "Crossing the Bar." Nearly every year someone would choose to do it. There would be absolute silence when the child would start, "Sunset and Evening Star and one clear call to me"—and then end it—"I hope to see my pilot face to face when I have crossed the bar." Some spoke lofty sayings. "A rolling stone gathers no moss"; "Heights by great men reached and kept were not attained by sudden flight"; "A living dog is better than a dead lion"; "Continually dripping wears a stone"; "Truth crushed to earth will rise again." Girls were not left out. With long blue or pink ribbons around their waists and done-up hair, they recited as well, their soft voices a contrast to the hoarse, changing voices of the boys.

Siblings singing together were always a hit. Their harmonious voices seemed to meld into one. Debates were held and could sometimes raise hackles like when the subject was "Did the South have a right to secede?" In his wisdom, Bud later made the debate a separate program and organized a debating society made up of adults. Some, it

was said, would walk six miles to participate on Friday nights. No subject was left without debate. They ranged from the trails of a coon dog
to the United States Constitution, to the Bible, law, medicine, and
even astronomy. One of the questions debated was whether the fear of
punishment would prompt a man to action quicker than the hope of
reward. The more Artemas learned, the more he realized that these
were not backward mountaineers in Choestoe, Georgia. They revered
and respected education. Choestoe was not just the "land of the dancing rabbits"; it was the valley of the "dancing minds".

The week had gone fast, and on Friday Artemas lingered for a
while at the school before heading back through Track Rock Gap. Bud
followed him outside to bid him farewell. "I hope the next time you
see me I've got a new Mrs. Miller to introduce you to," he confided.
When Artemas looked interested, he continued, "I've got my eye on
Jane Melinda Collins, one of Frank's girls. I'll soon be thirty-eight and
she's twenty-four." He grinned. "I'll have to put up with Bud, I guess."
He was referring to Jane's brother, Francis Jasper "Bud" Collins, the
colorful farmer and cattle trader of note who some years would make
5,000 gallons of sorghum syrup. He was known to have never worn a
store-bought piece of clothing, and once when he served as a state representative in Atlanta he wore a homemade shoe on one foot and an
Indian moccasin on the other. "Jane's like Bud, you know, she can get
tallow from an ant."

Artemas, remembering Jane, said, "She'll be worth it."

"That's for sure," Bud said, grinning again, "and I'll also get her
Uncle Tomp. You've heard about him, haven't you?" He saw that
Artemas had not. "Uncle Tomp is one of the most loved men in
Choestoe and one of its most interesting characters. His generosity
and love for his fellow man is well known.

"Once, about 1875, two men Tomp knew came to his house and
offered to hire him to take his mules and pull their loaded wagon to
the top of Tesnatee Gap. Their mules weren't up to such a haul. The
bargain was struck, and Tomp hitched his team up and the three
started out.

"Before they reached the Gap, federal revenue agents suddenly
appeared in the road. The two men jumped off the wagon and ran

into the woods. The wagon was loaded with moonshine liquor, and the agents offered not to make charges against Tomp if he would tell them the others' names. His response was 'Never.'

"So Thomp Collins was charged with possessing 'unstamped barrels' and sent to New York to prison. A couple of years went by, and the family did not hear from him. Many thought he was dead. Then one day he came walking into his front yard in Choestoe. He had walked every step of the way from New York. He told his wife, 'I've slept in many a fence corner and cut many a stick of wood for food. If ever a stranger comes by he is welcome to sleep in our house and share my food.'

"That's just one story; there are many. Once he was plowing in the field and a neighbor came and asked to borrow his mule, meaning when he got through. Tomp said, 'Wait until I get to the end of this row.' Another time, at the mill, someone asked for some meal. Tomp, who had just had his last bucket of corn ground, gave him his meal, slung his empty sack over his saddle horn, and went and bought a bushel for himself. Yes sir, I'll be honored to be part of that family."

Artemas could have listened to these Choestoe tales forever, but he had to get back to Brasstown Valley. So he thanked Bud for a most interesting week and asked one last question. Nodding his head toward the school, he inquired, "Where do they go when you've taught them all you know?"

Bud stared straight into his friend's eyes. "Ah, that's the question. You tell me?"

CHAPTER 11

Planting the Seed

As Artemas had made his way first from middle Georgia to Lincolnton, then to Dahlonega and over the mountains into Brasstown Valley, he became more convinced each day that this was a task Providence had been assigned him. He was glad he had spent the time with Elder Thomas in Dahlonega and renewed his spiritual strength from the Reverend Hamby. The Cokers and Bill Dean had been most helpful, but Artemas knew his work was just beginning. He prayed that God would give him the grace, grit, and gumption to plant this mustard seed of faith.

When he had first come into the settlement, he had noticed what appeared to be a store that was no longer being used. Bill Dean, who knew who owned what for miles around, told him it belonged to James Henry Stephens, the son of the woman who lived across the road from it, the widow of Dr. Judge Grimke Stephens.

The late Dr. Stephens had built a five-room house on the main road before the Civil War. In 1880, he had died from an injury suffered while on his way to see a patient in the Woodgrove settlement on the other side of the mountain. His horse had stumbled on the rough trail, and in trying to regain its footing, it reared and struck its head hard against Dr. Stephens's face. Although the doctor knew he was hurt badly, he continued on the steep grade over the Wagon Gap Mountain to the home of the sick man. There he went on to tend the patient but requested a bed as he was not able to return home. He died the next day.

Two years later in 1882, his widow, Nancy Louise Haynes Stephens, married William Mitchell Sanderson, a wealthy landowner from nearby Hayesville, North Carolina, whose parents had bought the land from the Indians. The Reverend Alfred E. Corn married them. Unfortunately, Mr. Sanderson died in a wagon accident within a couple of years, and Nancy Louise, now a wealthy widow for a second time, moved back to her home with their infant daughter Arry May.

Artemas went to see her about using the abandoned store across the muddy rutted road from where she was once again living. He found her to be an attractive, charming woman in her early forties, with an active and inquisitive mind. When Artemas told her about his dream of a school in the valley and his immediate project of finding a temporary location for classes to be held, she became the first person not to recoil or act shocked about such an audacious plan. Instead, she leaned forward in her chair and quickly spoke for her twenty-year-old son, "Henry will not be using that building anytime soon." She then talked about how it probably needed some cleaning and minor repairs, and she'd see that the work got done. As Artemas left floating on air, she followed him to the door and asked a question no one had ever asked him before: "How much land are you going to need for this school?"

That was an important question, and Artemas could only mutter, "We'll have to see." More important and more immediate was the one posed by Bill Dean earlier: "Where are the students?" One couldn't have a school without students. So the hunt began.

Except for one week when he went to Choestoe, much of the next six months were taken up with Artemas visiting the families who had children of school age and the movers and shakers of the area who could help him promote the school. He remembered the warning of Elder Thomas and repeated by Bill Dean that some families, fathers in particular, would feel they needed the children at home to help with the chores and that "learning" was a waste of time, especially for males.

Time and time again Bill Dean proved helpful. He knew where the families lived, and he had a good feel for what the response from both the father and the mother might be. More than once he advised that Artemas should try to talk with the mother first. Often he helped Artemas make out a list of prospects.

The Cokers were also helpful. And Mrs. Sanderson was supportive to the point of wanting to go with Artemas as he visited the families. On several occasions she did, usually when it seemed obvious to her that it would be the mother who made the decision.

Artemas grew to like this woman very much. A little more than ten years older than he, she was like the mother he had lost as a teenager. She carried herself almost regally and spoke softly but with authority. Sometimes Artemas worried that she would intimidate the other mountain women. Instead they were drawn to her and probably felt that, with some education, that's how their daughters might become.

Once when they were to visit a family on West Union, Mrs. Sanderson insisted they go in her buggy; Artemas would drive. The horse was spirited, and once when it began to act up, she quickly took the reins from Artemas, spoke sharply to the animal, and got it under control. Then she handed the reins back to Artemas without saying a word so he would be driving when they got to the house. They had gone to see a Mr. and Mrs. Logan, whom Bill Dean had said had a boy he knew would be interested, but they'd have to persuade his pa. "He ain't as big as a minute, just breath and britches, but there's something about him that's pretty special. I've watched how he listens to everything the grownups say," was how he described the boy.

The boy was out in the yard chopping wood when they arrived. He stopped quickly. He obviously had not seen a woman dressed as fine as Mrs. Stephens nor a buggy with a top on it. A woman in a bonnet and apron came to the door to see who the company was and then stepped out onto the porch. "You'uns come in," she said. Artemas somehow knew she was aware of who they were. *It's Mrs. Sanderson*, he thought, glad that she had come with him.

They entered a room with a ceiling even lower than most. A kettle was on the fireplace, and food was being prepared. Mrs. Sanderson wasted no time; Artemas had hardly introduced himself. "We want to talk with you about this here fine lad getting an education, going to a school that Reverend Lester is starting up in the settlement." Mrs. Sanderson was more refined than that; Artemas had never heard her say "this here boy," but immediately he understood that she wanted

Mrs. Logan to know that even though she had a five-room house and drove around in a fine buggy, she was not above the other woman, that she was of these mountains just like her. Mrs. Sanderson would explain on the way back, "Don't ever let someone think you think you're better than they are. These are proud people. Don't ever, ever do or say anything that might seem to put them down."

A day or so later Artemas went to see Bent Puett on Gum Log. This time he went alone. Mrs. Sanderson seemed to understand a woman talking to this man would do more harm than good. It was said Bent always carried a pistol. Once when asked why, he replied, "I've carried me one off'n on since I's a boy cuss I never wanted to be pushed around." James Benton Puett was born in Cherokee County, North Carolina, and had proudly served in the Union Army during the Civil War. He would be married three times and have eighteen children. His first wife named Bathsheba had died not long after Bent returned from the war. His second wife was Emily Jane Patton, and it was their children Artemas thought might be prospects. There were Sidney and Mae in particular, whom Artemas had heard were "bright as buttons." But Bent would have none of it. He was a proud man like Mrs. Sanderson had said and made it plain he needed no assistance from anybody in raising his children. Disappointed, Artemas could not help respecting this strong personality and was about to get back on his mule when Mr. Puett laid his hand on his shoulder and said, "Hold on, preacher. Would they learn their numbers or something worthwhile like that?" When assured they would, he thanked Reverend Lester for coming and said, "Now that would be good."

Artemas stayed on mule back constantly. It was a day in and day out grind for him and Beulah. He may not have been riding thousands of miles as the Wesleys and Asbury had, but he was covering Towns County from one end to the other as well as Union and some parts of North Carolina. During a two-week period, he visited Hog Creek, Bear Meat, Bell Creek, Hightower, and Barefoot. He also visited Bugscuffle, so named, one man said, because it was so poor even the bugs had to scuffle to keep alive. He went to the little settlement of Tree on the far west side of the county on the Rabun County line. He wanted to go all the way to Ellicott's Rock but figured it would take another week to make the journey, and he felt he didn't have that time to spare.

Ellicott's Rock was the large boulder used to designate the northeast corner of the state. In 1811, the famous surveyor, Major Andrew Ellicott of Lancaster, Pennsylvania, had been designated to determine what the true boundary was between Georgia and North Carolina. A dispute had been going on for years, and Georgia Governor David B. Mitchell wanted it settled. The rock was used to designate the 35th degree of North Latitude. Major Ellicott marked the rock with an "N" on one side, indicating North Carolina, and a "G" on the other side for Georgia.

Although Ellicott was considered the most accurate surveyor around and earlier had surveyed Georgia's southern boundary around 1800, it was later found he was off about 500 feet all across the new northern boundary, and Georgia's first Walton County was completely lost to North Carolina.

Visiting the post office in Tree was as far east as Artemas got. There he was entertained by the postmaster, Mr. Young, who was quite a yarn spinner and fiddler. As he was leaving, Young followed him out the door, fiddle in hand, asking, "Have you heard this'n?" The name of the post office was later changed to Tate City.

Artemas also visited Shake Rag, so named because during the Civil War some "shirkers" hid out in the Cedar Cliffs and came home when a white rag was put out to tell them they could return. Another small settlement was called "Scataway," where many made a living making whiskey. They would "scataway" when revenuers came around.

They were always changing names in the mountains. Little did Artemas know at that time, but even the name of the school he was working to start would be changed in only a few years.

The mountains were heavily wooded and sparsely populated; Artemas could ride for hours without seeing a living soul, but at the end of a three- or four-day trip when he counted up the names of the families he had visited, it would be twenty or more. He met the Crains and the Corns, the Dentons and the Taylors. An impressive young man he got to know, probably about age twenty, was Rome Burrell who would become the Towns County sheriff in a few years. He met the Wood and the Groves families. He met the Eller family, descendants of the Reverend Elisha Eller who had preached for many years at Persimmon Baptist just over the line in Rabun. He met the Berrong family and the Stonecyphers, whose ancestor, it was said, was with George Washington at Valley Forge. He met a man named Silas Dayton, said to be the strongest man in Hightower. One story was that he ran down a big buck deer in an open field where he held it by its antlers until someone came and killed it. They called him "Judge," and many came to seek his advice and allow him to settle disputes over property lines.

Artemas met Lucinda or "Cindy" and her husband "Big Jim" Arrowood. He met the Kendalls on Fodder Creek and got to spend time with Uriah "Dick" Gibson, who had a full white beard and had been a justice of the peace on Bell Creek going back to the time of the Civil War.

One of the most impressive was a schoolteacher and Baptist preacher named Elijah Kimsey who looked to Artemas like an Old Testament prophet. Years later Artemas would remember meeting this great uncle of Dr. George W. Truett when he read that Truett, then a renowned Baptist minister in Dallas, Texas, called Kimsey "the most powerful and irresistible exhorter he had ever heard."

These powerful old-time preachers fascinated young Artemas, who envied their ability to move their congregations. In his first year in the pulpit in Lincolnton, Artemas had used a sermon outline he had laboriously prepared and had carried that practice with him to the mountains. He quickly saw that it did not work well on this circuit. That was especially true with the Baptists, he noted. For many, a prepared sermon meant that it was the man who was speaking; while an extemporaneous sermon, they felt, gave God the opportunity to speak *through* the preacher. It was then, the congregation felt, that God had truly called this man to preach. If this did not happen and the preacher was slow or tongue-tied, then the verdict was the Lord had not truly called him. Some preachers would open their sermons with the disclaimer, "I never learned how to preach, I never tried to learn how to preach." Some would say they just "talked around" waiting for the "revelation."

One "relevated" or "quickened" their mode of delivery when they felt the spirit of God moving them and giving them the words. The delivery then became a chanted style, and the cadences would rise and fall with the passions of the preacher. Short sentences were rhythmically delivered with an explosion of exhaling or inhaling air at the end of a sentence, "haah." It was not the monotonous tone Artemas had heard from so many preachers, including himself. It was a melody of the purist nature, almost poetic in expression. It was a climax that was gradually built up until the point when many believed the Lord was speaking through the preacher. At times the words could become almost unintelligible to an unfamiliar ear, and it took Artemas a while to get used to it. It was God-given native eloquence. "Twasn't studied" was how one admiring listener put it. Often the congregation would also "get the spirit" and join in. The women would shout or "praise" and the men embrace each other, sometimes even getting up into the pulpit and hugging the preacher as he continued to preach.

Among the pioneer families of Towns County were three Taylor brothers, Jeremiah, John, and Andrew Jackson, who moved into the Owl Creek area shortly after the Cherokees were removed. Jeremiah served in the Confederate Army and saw combat at Missionary Ridge and Chickamauga, where he was wounded. He named one of his sons Robert E. Lee Taylor. Artemas visited some of the Taylor family around Soapstone Gap and found them highly intelligent and musically and mechanically inclined.

While up in that area of the county, he also got to know Oliver Cromwell Wyly, whose father had built three inns along the Unicoi Turnpike. There the weary traveler could get food and shelter, and while he might have to share a bed with a stranger, it was better than sleeping on the ground or in the back of a wagon. The trail ran from Augusta, Georgia, to Tellico Plains, Tennessee, a distance of 180 miles. In Towns County it was called the Wyly Road. It came through Unicoi Gap at the crest of the Blue Ridge that separated Towns and White counties. Unicoi is a Cherokee word meaning "white." A few miles north of the gap at the headwaters of the Hiawassee River, Wyly had built in 1820 the first brick home in the mountains using his slaves for labor, and then gave two of them as payment to the main builder.

In 1852, Wyly had donated land along the Hiawassee River for the Mt. Zion Methodist Episcopal Church. Artemas preached there each month and afterward, as was the custom, had a wonderful meal in that beautiful brick house then owned by the Ezekiel Brown family.

One week he visited George Washington Swanson on Crooked Creek right at the North Carolina state line. Artemas had heard he was a strong Christian who had helped start the Woodgrove Baptist Church and a few years before had lost an infant daughter, Zady. When Artemas arrived, a new daughter had just been born, Ila Elizabeth. They placed her in a cradle, the one Zady had used a few years before. "It's made out of buckeye," George announced proudly. "It's pretty wood, don't you think, and easy to work with it's so light. When Zady was a baby, Mama would rock with her foot and churn at the same time, just slow and steady with the evening breeze." His eyes were misty, and even with the new baby, one could see he still missed Zady.

Time stood still in more ways than one for the early pioneer mountaineer. Few had clocks or watches and most told time either by means of homemade sundials or calculating the positions of the sun by day and the stars by night. Months and years were measured in the number of moons, temperatures were calculated by the course and density of the clouds, and the weather in general was predicted by the direction and velocity of the wind and actions of the birds and animals that were part of their everyday lives. They studied the growth of wild plants to guide them in the planting and harvesting of their crops. The possession of an almanac was valued only slightly less than that of the essential squirrel rifle and the revered family Bible. The family that possessed all three plus a skillet and iron pot considered itself well off indeed.

The center of life of the mountain family was its cabin—a rough but sturdy structure built of notched logs with flattened inner and outer faces and chinked with clay from nearby dirt banks. This abode started out as one large single room with a sleeping loft for the children, a big stone chimney at one end, and a single sash for a window at the other. A narrow porch usually was added on the front, and a small lean-to was sometimes built at the rear for a kitchen. As the family grew and prospered, a second room about the same size of the cabin would be added, and the two connected by an open hallway called a "dog trot." The building was topped off with a single-gabled roof covered with hand-split oak shingles fastened in place at first with wooden pegs and later by short, square-shaped nails. Split-log puncheons were used to cover the floors of the earlier cabins and later were replaced by rough planks that were more sightly but less durable. The family was perceived to have achieved great prosperity when its members added a second floor to the house with rooms similar to those below. Only a few homes were as nice as the Wyly home on The River and the Sanderson home in Brasstown Valley.

Of all the many things the cabins lacked, privacy would be at the top of the list. Families of sometimes as many as seven brothers and an equal number of sisters shared the meager amenities with their parents and often one or more of their grandparents. All of them ate, slept, and performed their ablutions mostly in the presence and sight of the others, often to the embarrassment of visitors who had to do likewise. Most slept in their daytime clothes or underwear, always several to a bed, assuring warmth in winter and varying degrees of body odors in all seasons. The same homemade lye soap used for the laundry was also used for the bath. Outdoor privies were more the exception than the rule for many years, and calls of nature were answered behind the nearest tree or in the barn. Some used buckets, but only the very affluent had the luxury of a chamber pot or "slop jar."

The heart of the mountain cabin was its fireplace, which took up most of one end of the structure and served the residents with fire for heat, light, and cooking. A fire was kept burning, if no more than just hot coals ready for stoking, at all times, and the family too poor to own a prized hoard of matches was careful to see that it never went out. If it did, a family member, usually one of the children, would have to be dispatched to the home of the nearest neighbor to "borry some far."

Another unique feature of the mountain home was the ash hopper, a triangular trough cut in a small log, one end of which was raised a few inches, and a frame set on four posts in the ground with its peak in the trough. Ashes from the fireplace or kitchen stove, if the cabin had one, were poured into the hopper, which was kept covered until the woman of the house determined it was soap-making time. She then poured water over the ashes and collected the resulting lye that trickled through the trough. It was boiled in a big kettle with pieces of fat meat or collected accumulations of kitchen drippings until it formed a soft brown substance that, when dried, was cut into pieces and used as lye soap for both laundry and family baths. Often, they washed clothes down at the creek and used a "battlin' block" to get the dirt loose.

Dishes were rare in the early mountain household. Wooden "trenchers" and dressed boards were used in place of china, and gourds of all sizes and shapes were utilized as substitutes for cups, bowls, and glasses as well as for containers of lard, sugar, salt, soap, syrup, molasses, seed, and any other household substances that needed storing. Every family equipped its spring with a drinking gourd fastened by a leather thong or piece of twine to a nearby bush. However poor and destitute mountain people might be, they never were given to self-pity. Artemas never met a mountain beggar, and the first and last word on the subject of handouts or charity was "We-un's ain't that hard pushed yit."

September soon turned into October with a glorious burst of color. "A picture no artist could paint" was how Mrs. Sanderson had put it. First would come the red of the sourwood and then toward the end of the month the yellows of the poplars, hickories, and chestnuts, and then the tapestry of God's handiwork was complete. When the first frost fell, the prickly burrs on the huge chestnuts opened and the chestnuts began to fall to the ground. Artemas watched in amazement as one could pick up a gallon of the tasty nuts in only a few minutes. The trees were huge, at least eighty or ninety feet high, and almost as wide where they could spread their branches. Families would take a wagon and go into the woods close to a "good stand" and in one afternoon fill their wagon full. The nuts could be eaten raw, boiled, or roasted. The Cherokees used them in bread.

It was also the time of the year the men would notice the "signs"—how thick the shucks of corn, the bark on a tree, the fur on an animal—which would foretell the severity of the coming winter. "Nature has her way," they would say, "and there ain't nothing you can do about it."

Artemas remembered back to that cold January day he came through Track Rock and forded Brasstown Creek into Towns County. He remembered looking back at Double Knobs and Brasstown Bald. He had watched the mountains turn green and seen the rainbows from the summer rains. The Cherokees had called their rainbows "Thunder God's Bow." And then the season turned from gold and red to gray. Soon the forests were naked and it was hog-killing time.

Bill Dean enlisted Artemas to help with one. It was an all-day job that began with building fires and boiling water at the freezing first light of dawn and finished with grinding and stuffing the sausage and hanging the dressed meat in the smokehouse in the failing light of dusk.

Once the water was boiling in a half dozen or so borrowed cast-iron wash pots, half the men would proceed to dispatch the hog while the remainder poured the boiling water into a huge barrel usually half buried on a slant in the ground as near as possible to the hog pen. Artemas watched as Bill fed the animal some corn to distract him and then dropped him with one blow to the head with the blunt end of an axe. When the hog fell, one of the men jumped into the pen and slashed his throat with a razor-sharp butcher knife so all the blood could run out before it congealed.

When the bleeding was complete, the men then knocked down the side of the pen, manhandled the carcass onto a board or mule-pulled drag, and pulled it to the vat where, using a singletree and a block and tackle, they then maneuvered it into the bubbling water. Once the scalding was completed, the carcass was lifted high by the hind legs, and the scraping commenced until all the hair was removed and the skin was smooth and shiny white.

While still hanging, the carcass was disemboweled with great care taken not to puncture any of the internal organs and thus taint the meat. Women then suddenly appeared with pans from the kitchen ready to receive such delicacies as the heart, liver, pancreas or "melt" as it was called, and then some for those who relished the lungs or "lights." One woman placed the small intestines in a washtub and carried it a distance downwind where it was cleaned and prepared to be chitlins or use as sausage casings.

Bill Dean was everywhere, giving orders what to do next, or maybe he was just showing off for Artemas. The empty carcass was stretched out on a cutting table made of boards suspended across sawhorses, and the "cutting up" begin—first the head and then the hams, belly and sides, ribs and backbone. When the ribs and backbone were reached, the tenderloin was removed and taken by one of the watching children to the kitchen where it would be fried and served later with hot biscuits and milk pan gravy for the traditional "hog-killing day" dinner. Being very perishable, the tenderloin always was consumed on the day of the killing.

Artemas noticed that all of the pieces were trimmed closely and carefully, and the lean trimmings were piled in pans for sausage and the fat placed in a washtub to be boiled down for lard and cracklins that afternoon by the women. The hams were rubbed with salt and hung in the smokehouse as were the shoulders. The head, after the brains were removed for serving with eggs for the next day's breakfast, and the feet were saved for making "sousemeat" or "head cheese" after being boiled to release the gelatin that would hold it together when fashioned into a loaf.

Some of the belly fat was saved for bacon, and the streak-o-lean of the sides was cut into slabs and salted down for curing in the bins of the smokehouse. The chitlins had been cleaned and rinsed and re-rinsed and were now soaked in a weak lye solution. Later they would be fried and eaten as a special delicacy. Some were stretched out and cut into stuffing lengths to be used to hold the sausage.

The ribs and backbone were cut up and divided among the participants in the "killing" and were destined to be boiled as meals for their families during the coming week.

It was mid-afternoon when the sausage mill was brought out and the grinding, seasoning, and stuffing of the meat began. The children were pressed into service to turn the handles of the grinders.

Usually two kinds of sausage were mixed—extra hot with a lot of pepper for the menfolks and a milder version for the womenfolks. Once stuffed in the casings or chitlins, both ends were tied, and they were rubbed with salt and spices and also hung in the smokehouse to cure with the hams and bacon. Since they cured faster than the others, they were the first of the cured meat to be available for the table later in the winter. But for those who liked their sausage strong, the last and most dried-out links were by far the best, even if they did have to be soaked before they were soft enough to be cooked.

Artemas had not received the official word about his next year's assignment, but Elder Thomas had sent word that he probably would be moved. At first he had been disappointed and surprised. He had found a site and he had hunted students for six months. He had studied the school in Choestoe and had given some thought as to how this one should be conducted. He felt cheated of his chance, but then, as was his way, after more careful consideration and some deep prayer, he realized they needed a more experienced teacher than he. He had no experience as a teacher, and in the back of his head he held out hope that maybe he would be sent to a city, a place where he could find a wife perhaps. As he prepared to leave the following Monday, he made a list in his head of those he must thank: the Cokers, Bill Dean, the Logans whom he felt sure would send John, that bright son of theirs, and, of course Mrs. Sanderson. *What would I have done without her?* Artemas thought. *She was the answer to my prayer.* He would go by and see his friends in Choestoe and urge them to support the school. And, without a doubt, stop in Dahlonega and make sure with Elder Thomas that the institute would be named for Bishop Holland Nimmon McTyeire and, if possible, rename the post office McTyeire. *That would really make my year up here worthwhile,* he concluded.

It would be a long ride back for him and Beulah, but before he left Artemas had one last sermon to preach in Brasstown Valley.

The Seed Sprouts

Years later, one of the school's original students, John G. Logan, remembered the first day of class that was held a few weeks after Artemas had left:

Well do I remember that momentous Monday in January 1886 when I set out to realize my life's ideal. I rejoice today, more than ever, that on this first Monday morning I lent my influence and presence in starting off dear old Young Harris. The sun was shining beautifully that morning. The road was frozen several inches deep, and when thawed was almost impassable. I made this one and one-half mile journey on foot.

The "automobile" of those days was an ordinary horse and buggy or an old-time ox wagon. It was nothing unusual for the front axle to scrape the road. Walking was preferable.

Old Cedar and Double Knobs were in their glory that morning. Draped in their polar ermine they seemed to smile upon a lonely lad on his way to gratify the highest ambition of his young heart.

Our small clan soon gathered. I say "clan" advisedly, for Young Harris students are noted the world over for their brotherly love for each other. The very day this institution of learning was born this spirit of love also came into being. God grant that it may never die!

Enrolled that first morning were Ida Stephens, John G. Logan, Will T. Hunt, Elijah Morgan, Sallie Erwin, Bill Daniel, and Candice Matheson.

The old-fashioned wood fire, glowing from the old-time fireplace, gave us a royal welcome that frosty morning. The storehouse about which we have heard so much these years gone by, where Young Harris was started, had two small rooms, with a porch on the front jutting close upon the big road. Our educational equipment consisted of a few rickety chairs and two or three uncomfortable benches.

While Logan named the original seven students who attended the first day of class, others came and went that first year. Some days there would be as few as four and at other times as many as twenty.

Artemas, of course, was not there that first year the school was in operation. He had planted the seed and moved on to his next assignment in Rome. That would be his history, and Rome would be the largest city in which he pastored.

The man chosen to replace him to become the first principal and sole teacher was the Reverend Marcus Hale Edwards from LaFayette, up in Walker County in the northwest corner of the state. He was called "Mark" and was thirty-eight years old. He had taught for three years before becoming a Methodist minister. He was the son of very active churchgoing parents and had been converted at an early age. When he was twenty-six years old in 1874, he married Elizabeth Hill. Their first child, a son, had died at an early age, and the death made a deep impression on him. Always a pious man, he felt the Lord called him to do something special. For three years he preached in the Coosawattee mission, mostly in Fairmont. When Elder Thomas suggested his going to the new school in the mountains, he jumped at the opportunity. The Cokers helped Mark and Elizabeth find a place to live near them within easy walking distance to the school. For the next two years Mark taught five days a week for seven months and also preached twice on Sundays. He also continued combing the area for students. In doing so he found a major challenge: competition Artemas had not expected. But he also found a benefactor who had the desire, the goodness, the resources, and the credibility to make a huge difference.

The immense challenge arose just over Brasstown Mountain where stiff competition for the new school was developing in Hayesville, North Carolina, and Hiawassee, Georgia. The one in Hayesville was another school that had been going on for several years. Early on it had been called Hicksville Academy, founded, named, and operated by Professor John O. Hicks, who was highly respected and known to be an able teacher, strong disciplinarian, and good organizer. Just the year before in 1885, a promising local mountain lad of eighteen completed ten years of studies there and immediately set up another school on Crooked Creek in Georgia right across the state line. His name was George W. Truett, and within a few years he would become one of the most respected Baptist preachers in the world. He had about thirty students at his school ranging from seven to twenty years of age. Truett did so well that in 1886 he moved his school to Hiawassee, where he joined with his cousin to start an academy there. His cousin was from the respected McConnell family and was already highly regarded as a preacher. His mane was Fernando "Ferd" C. McConnell, and he was ten years older than Truett. He immediately supported the idea and gave the academy his considerable assistance. So as McTyeire Institute was struggling to get off the ground, these two young charismatic cousins were providing considerable competition. It became a Baptist-Methodist tug of war. And there were many more Baptists than Methodists.

Hiawassee Academy began operation in the Towns County courthouse in January 1887 with tuition one dollar a month for all grades. No one who desired admission was turned away, even if they could not pay at the time. George W. Truett was principal for two and a half years, January 1887 to June 1889. During that short period the enrollment grew to 300 students, which included 23 young Baptist preachers and 51 public school teachers who came to the academy for further training. It was going like a house on fire.

George W. Truett was then twenty-four years old, and already few, if any, could match his speaking ability. Dr. J. B. Hawthorne, pastor of the First Baptist Church of Atlanta and one of the great pulpit orators of all time, heard Truett make an appeal for funds for the academy at the Georgia Baptist Convention in 1887, where he electrified the crowd. Hawthorne described it this way: "I have heard Henry W. Grady, the South's most brilliant orator. I have heard Henry Ward Beecher and Phillips Brooks and others of the world's most famous speakers, but never in my life has my soul been stirred by any speaker as it was that day in Marietta by that boy out of the mountains. My heart burned within me and I could not keep back the tears."

Others were just as impressed. One wealthy businessman in attendance offered to pay for Truett to attend Mercer University, but the mountain lad did not accept it. Instead, in the summer of 1889, Truett left the mountains of his birth and followed his parents, Charles and Rebecca Truett, and his brother out west to Whitewright, Texas. At that time he hoped to become a lawyer. But the local church discovered his speaking and teaching talents, made him their Sunday school superintendent, and urged him to become a preacher. Finally, George W. Truett, raised in the shadow of Tusquittee Bald, made that decision, and his future would be unlimited.

But the good Lord above can look after more than one person or thing at a time. As He was looking after the Baptist George W. Truett, so He was also looking after the Methodist Marcus H. Edwards. About a hundred miles from Brasstown Valley in Clarke County, at the First Methodist Church of Athens, its pastor, George Yarborough, had heard from his friend Elder Thomas in Dahlonega about the Methodist school being started in Brasstown Valley.

Instantly, Reverend Yarborough thought of his church's most generous member, Judge Young L. G. Harris, who it was said had never turned down a solicitation when it came to Christian education, even contributing to the construction of a Christian school in Shanghai, China. He had been the Sunday school superintendent for nearly forty years, and he and Mrs. Harris had no children.

As expected, the Judge was interested, but like the attorney and good businessman he was, he wanted more information about it. At that time Judge Harris was in his mid-seventies and his wife, Susan, was not in good health. He would have liked to "eyeball" the place and see for himself its potential and need, but under the circumstances, he knew he could not. So, as on many other occasions, he turned to his business assistant and close friend, Colonel W. W. Thomas, to make a trip to the mountains. His instructions were to determine the need, select a site "that will have room for growth," and ascertain what buildings early on would be needed.

Thomas was a man who got things done. He took the ideas and orders from others and made them work. And he dearly loved a challenge, the bigger and more complicated the better. He had also heard of the infant school from one of his relatives, Elder A. C. Thomas in Dahlonega. So when the colonel got his marching orders, he was anxious to go, even though he knew it would be a long, difficult trip.

He traveled up the old Unicoi Turnpike, which followed old Indian trails that had been there for hundreds of years before the white man ever came. In 1716 Colonel George Chicken traveled it and commented that he "had to walk more than he rode." Particularly hard, he regarded, was the trail between Chota in the Nacoochee Valley and the Cherokee settlement of Quo-neoshee over Unicoi Gap.

In 1886, a hack pulled by two good mules could make twenty miles a day, and Colonel Thomas was able to make Brasstown Valley in five days. It was still wild country, and the one night the colonel had to spend outside on the ground, he heard the howls of wolves and once, he thought, the scream of a panther or "painter" as the mountain men called them. The lush virgin forests with trees of unbelievable size also struck him. The driver for the last half of the journey was a man named England whose family had come to the area in the 1830s and stayed around the gold fields and Mossy Creek. He said his grandmother, Margaret, had won a land lot in the 1832 Gold Lottery. Later she went on over the mountains into Choestoe and was the first woman to be buried in the old Choestoe Baptist cemetery.

Thomas spent his last night on the road in the Wyly Inn at the foot of the mountain after coming through Unicoi Gap. He had a good night's sleep, was up early, and got into Hiawassee early in the afternoon the next day. Quietly, he had someone show him the courthouse where the Hiawassee Academy was beginning to attract a number of students. Like the good businessman he was, he wanted to see the competition. He then went through Brasstown Gap, or Wagon Gap as it was called then, and for the first time looked down on Brasstown Valley. Like so many others, before him and since, he was staggered by the beauty and grandeur. It took his breath away. Arriving at the school, the colonel found Reverend Mark Edwards waiting on him. They talked until almost dark and ate supper across the road with Mrs. Sanderson. Thomas spent the night in her spacious house, and it was good to be off the road. His body still felt like it was swaying and rocking from being in the hack for most of the week.

The next morning he looked around the area. They first went to the site that Artemas had been sold on from the beginning. It was on the Towns County side of Brasstown Creek where Artemas had looked toward Mount Enotah and rejoiced in the beauty of that mountain stretching toward heaven. When Colonel Thomas saw the land, he too was impressed and said, "This is it; can we buy it?"

That turned out to be more difficult than expected. Two acres were easily bought, and Thomas was so sure he could get the rest and was in such a hurry to get back to Athens, he even had some building material delivered to the site. Unfortunately, the owner of the surrounding land, William W. "Buck" Erwin, knowing its potential for farming, would not budge. It had been Erwin property since the 1850s when Robert Houston Erwin, one of the Valley's earliest pioneers, had brought his family from Burke County, North Carolina. Colonel Thomas, knowing two acres was not enough, began to look elsewhere. It turned out to be right under his nose from where he was staying at the Sanderson house.

He had hit it off immediately with the widow. Like Artemas, Mark Edwards, and the others, Colonel Thomas was impressed with the spirit and common sense of this remarkable woman. She seemed to be as disappointed as he and Mark when not enough land could be purchased at the Brasstown Creek site.

One morning, as the two were having an early breakfast before he began another day's search, Mrs. Sanderson surprised him by saying, almost in a whisper, "Let's quit looking. You can have that property I own right up the hill. Or at least ten acres of it. Will that do?"

Colonel Thomas almost spilled his coffee as he was about to take a sip. He rose to his feet to hug her but quickly thought that wouldn't be proper, so he just stood there looking down on this generous, unusual woman. It hit him that this must be how Artemas felt when she had told him he could use the store for the first classes.

Quickly, he got up with Mark Edwards, and the three went to look at the site, which was only about 300 yards from the home of Mrs. Sanderson. It was where the old Oak Forrest Methodist Church had once stood before being moved a few miles away. The small church had been "quartered," cut in four pieces, and hauled to a site across the county line where it was reassembled and renamed Zion Methodist Church in the 1870. The land of Mrs. Sanderson was perfect, right at the foot of Double Knobs; Crow Gap and old Cedar to the east and Three Sisters Mountain to the west, Brasstown Bald hidden behind Granny Knob. And it was practically on the main road coming through the settlement. He knew Judge Harris would be pleased with this report and could hardly wait to get back to Athens and tell him.

Shortly after he left, Nancy Louise married her third husband, Virgil L. Robertson, with Reverend Edwards performing the ceremony. On November 11, 1886, the deed for the property was finalized, and in the March term 1887, the Towns County Superior Court made it official.

At that same spring court in 1887, the biggest murder trial in the history of the young county was held. A few months before in December, a man named Tilman Justice had murdered a James G. Goddard in the Tate City area. Justice thought Goddard had reported him for making whiskey, and when he saw him coming across an open field, Justice shot him. He was tried, found guilty, and sentenced to hang the next month. The sheriff of Towns County at that time was R. P. (Pince) Burch, and it was his duty to carry out the sentence. Hundreds came from miles around to "the hanging ground" right off the Hiawassee square near the river. Many got there the night before for a good viewing place. The man to be hanged had only one arm, and on the gallows he held his baby as the noose was being placed around his neck. He had pleaded for two hours to the sheriff that he be spared. After pulling the "trigger" to the drop door, Sheriff Burch, a non-drinking man, was said to have drunk a gallon of whiskey, he was so unnerved. From the time the murder happened to the time of the trial was three months; from the time of the guilty verdict to the execution was less than a month. Swift justice, swift punishment.

The board of missions of the Methodist Church could not meet their hoped-for appropriation in 1887, but they sent a few hundred dollars. Other gifts were coming in, more property was purchased, and the first college building was completed before the year ended. Enrollment reached seventy-five students, and they were not all

coming just from the mountain area. Judge Harris was largely responsible for that as he was telling his friends all over the state about this
new school.

At the spring term in 1888, the Superior Court granted the charter, and as stated the school's purpose was ". . . the establishment,
maintenance and operation of a college of Liberal Arts to give, promote and extend instruction and education in any and all branches of
learning and education literary, mechanical, theological or otherwise
as may be desired or deemed proper . . . ."

On July 25, 1888, the board of the newly named Young L. G.
Harris Institute held its first meeting in the principal's office on the
institute campus. Trustees present were the men who had petitioned
for the charter: Chairman A. C. Thomas, presiding elder of the
Dahlonega District; Methodist ministers W. F. Robison and Edward
A. Gray; Wier Boyd; B. W. Coleman; J. D. Cooley; and Helm Hunt.
Judge Young L. G. Harris did not attend the board meeting, but a
letter from him stating his views on the new institute was read.
Reverend Edwards, desiring to return to active ministry, submitted his
letter of resignation, and the Reverend Edward A. Gray, who had just
become reassociated with the Conference after spending four years as
a missionary to the Cherokees, was elected his successor as principal.

He was authorized to charge $1.00 per month for tuition. The
trustees also appointed a committee to investigate the property of the
institute and offer a report at the next day's session.

A part of the report read as follows:

We find the land whereon the Institute is located is composed of
sixty acres well selected in the beautiful valley of Brasstown in Towns
County, Georgia—having all the advantages of good water, and
attractive scenery, highly conducive to health and happiness.

On this land there is already constructed eleven tenements,
including the main building, mostly used and occupied as dormito-
ries for students. The main building is well constructed, being sixty
feet long, by forty feet wide; two stories high, with two rooms below
and six rooms above, to which is added a dwelling house for
Principal, a dining room and kitchen. These are well furnished with
good spring water by iron pipes. We find a bell erected on a tempo-

rary structure, but a permanent one is in process of erection. A laundry is being fitted up with all the modern appointments of conveniences, etc.

In 1889, the Reverend C. C. Spence, an Emory graduate and a former cavalryman in the Confederate Army, was elected principal, and the board changed his title to that of president. A policy was adopted allowing school property to be leased to persons interested in "patronizing the institute" on which they could erect small houses where their sons and daughters could live while attending classes.

Also that year, attempts were made to move the new school to the nearby town of Blairsville. This was vetoed by the board as was a similar proposal that the institute unite with Hayesville College at Hayesville, North Carolina.

The Towns County Superior Court in 1891 approved an amendment to the charter empowering the institute to confer diplomas. The first graduates of Young L. G. Harris College were Lala Simpson and Ida Stephens of McTyeire, W. S. Sanders of Danielsville, and Beulah Watkins of Gainesville. They received the A. B. Degree. Ida was the daughter of Mrs. Nancy Louise Sanderson.

The mountain citizens of McTyeire were proud of their new college and in 1892 received permission from the postal authorities to change the name of the post office to Young Harris. The post office had been moved from near Track Rock to a site adjacent to the college property. The town of Young Harris was incorporated December 5, 1895. The city limits were one-half mile in every direction from the Susan B. Harris Chapel on the campus of the college.

Judge Harris had donated 260 additional acres of land in 1892 and set aside $160 for the purchase of another tract of land near the school. In 1888, at a cost of approximately $5,000, he had constructed the first permanent building on the Young Harris College campus. It was a brick chapel erected in the memory of his wife Susan who had recently passed away. He specified that it was to be used as a permanent place of worship for both students and community people. Thus was organized the Young Harris Methodist Church.

Enrollment had jumped to an astounding 400 students by 1892. The commencement speaker that year was the great orator and preacher Sam P. Jones of Cartersville. He attracted a huge crowd, some traveling more than 40 miles in covered wagons or oxcarts to hear him.

Reverend Spence served as president until 1894 and then was transferred to churches in nearby White and Lumpkin counties. Later, he established J. S. Green College in Demorest, Georgia, which eventually became Piedmont College. Another Confederate Army veteran, the Reverend William F. Robison, took his place and served for five years. He had been a member of the first board. With Robison's leadership, the college not only survived but continued to grow and improve. Modern plumbing was installed in the girls' dormitory; all the buildings were covered with handmade shingles.

Judge Harris died during this period, and there was great uncertainty as to whether the school could survive without this great benefactor who had continued to make annual contributions to the school. The general impression was that the school could not carry on without his assistance. An estimate of the financial contributions of Judge Harris to the college would be difficult to determine because the institution kept no records of receipts or disbursements during the first two years of existence. During his lifetime, he gave funds for the purchase of approximately 400 acres of land and, upon his death in 1894, left the college fifty shares of capital stock in the Atlanta and West Point Railroad Company, twenty-five shares of capital stock in the Georgia Railroad and Banking Company, and $5,000 in cash.

Though Judge Harris never visited the site of the college that bore his name, he made his views known through correspondence to its board of trustees. In a letter to the board in 1890 he set forth his philosophy of the college: "I am for accommodating first of all the people in the section around our school. If we can do that and then have room for the regions beyond, very well, but first of all let us keep well in hand and in heart the interest of the people who live in that section of the state."

In another letter, Judge Harris regretted he could not be present for a meeting of the board and added in his typical modest way, "You are all more familiar with the situation and the necessities of the institute than I am and I feel perfectly satisfied to leave its interest in your hands."

In 1895, the Reverend Sam Jones again preached on Commencement Sunday and again drew an overflow crowd estimated at 2,000. People came from forty miles away to hear the speech in the brush arbor next to the campus. Toward the end of his speech, a baby began to cry loudly. The mother continued to hold the baby, and the baby continued to cry. Finally, Reverend Jones brought his speech to an end with this comment, "When I'm feeling well, I can out holler a baby. I'm not feeling that well today, and I'm afraid that baby has won." The next year Jones became a member of the college board of trustees, where his enormous reputation proved to be an asset in attracting students.

But even with this, all was not well with the infant institute. The gifts from Judge Harris had been primarily in land and buildings, and there was a struggle to make ends meet in operating the college. Especially troubling was the inability to pay the faculty. The president's salary was $750 a year, and teachers earned an average of $400 a year. The entire faculty payroll was $3200.

The board of trustees requested financial help with this from the Methodist board of missions, but nothing came of the request. Towns County did chip in $200 from their limited budget to help with the lower grades. Just when things looked their worst, the board was asked to come to Athens to meet in the offices of the Southern Mutual Insurance Company. The stock bequest of Judge Harris had appreciated considerably. There was $8,571.25 in cash. Judge Harris was still smiling down from heaven.

Even with that, the struggle for operating funds continued. In 1899, W. F. Robison retired as president but remained as a faculty member for a few months. Professor J. W. Boyd acted as president, and then Reverend Joseph Astor Sharp was appointed. It would prove to be a marriage made in heaven between a man and a college.

CHAPTER 13

The Man Young Harris

After the British captured Savannah in 1778, Georgia's government reorganized in Augusta, and then, after a fierce battle, it too fell. Two Harris brothers, Walter and David, fought in the siege of Augusta. They were of Welsh decent, their ancestors coming to America right after the Glorious Revolution in 1688. David was killed and buried in Augusta; Walter ended up in nearby Greene County. His son, Walter Harris, Jr., then married an Athens girl, Virginia Billups, and settled in southern Clarke County, where they had eleven children.

One of their seven sons was Young Loften Gerdine Harris, born in 1812 the year our second war with Britain started. He graduated from the University of Georgia, studied law, and at the age of twenty-two was admitted to the Bar. He moved to nearby Elberton to start his practice. Called Elbertville in the beginning, the city and county were named in honor of the Revolutionary War hero and Indian fighter Samuel Elbert.

Geographically, it was an ideal location for agriculture, not too hot in the summer or too cold in the winter, free from storms and floods, and it had rich, fertile soil. The only thing that was considered a nuisance by some landowners and farmers was the outcroppings and boulders strewn over the countryside. In 1882, the first of what would be many granite quarries began to appear.

Even in the 1830s, the Indian menace was still real. In 1822 a band of hostile Cherokees raided the area and killed a family. The year that Harris began law practice in 1834, one of the county's prominent citizens and Indian agent, General Wiley Thompson, was killed in Florida by the famed chief of the Seminoles, Osceola. Thompson had represented the county in the state legislature and the U.S. Congress and had first served as an Indian agent under Andrew Jackson.

The man immortalized in the song "Old Dan Tucker" for years was one of Elbert county's best-known citizens. A minister, he had owned a large plantation and operated a ferry on the Savannah River for many years in the early 1800s.

The area was rich in religious history. Francis Asbury, the Methodist bishop and circuit rider, sponsored the first Methodist Annual Conference in 1788 at Thompson's Meeting House, later known as Bethlehem Methodist Church.

It was a place that valued education. In 1823, the legislature incorporated Eudisco Academy, and three years later the Elberton Female Academy, only the second female school in the state, was opened.

The young lawyer was in the county less than two years when he met and married Susan Beverly Allen, the granddaughter of one of the pioneers of the county, William Allen, who came to the area in 1756. William had two sons, Beverly, named after his brother, and Singleton Wathall.

Both brothers had represented Elbert County in the Georgia House of Representatives and Georgia Senate. Susan's sister, Marie Louise, married William McPherson McIntosh, who also served in both houses of the Georgia legislature and became Harris's law partner in Elberton. So Harris and McIntosh were not only brothers-in-law and law partners but were also married into the leading political and business family in the area, a family that was also connected by marriage to one of the early governors of Georgia, Stephen Heard.

The legend of Beverly Allen, Susan's great uncle, covered the Upper Savannah River country and particularly Elbert County like a quilt covers a bed. And when Young Harris married into the Allen family, he became part of that legacy whether he planned it that way or not.

Beverly Allen had once been a spell-binding Methodist preacher. He had accompanied Asbury on some of his travels, carried on an extended correspondence with John Wesley and was a close friend of the Reverend Peter Cartwright. Then something happened. In 1791, Bishop Asbury expelled Allen from the Methodist church for "immorality" and mentioned a "flagrant crime." The exact reason was never made clear. Everyone knew Asbury tolerated no dissent, and it could have been church politics between two strong-willed personalities. Earlier Asbury had written that Allen was "writing to Mr. Wesley" and "creating mischief."

Whatever it was, Beverly Allen came to Elbert County and went into the mercantile business with his brother William, who had also opened a tavern on the road to Petersburg. At that time, Petersburg was the third largest city in the state and an important port city on the Savannah River where it intersected with the Broad River. Exactly what happened next is lost in the murkiness of history, as is much of the Beverly Allen story, but it seems the Allen brothers got overextended in their businesses and several lawsuits were brought against them by creditors.

Whatever the situation, in January 1794, U.S. Marshall Robert Forsyth approached the Allen brothers on the first floor of a boarding house in Augusta to serve them warrants. They both fled, Beverly running to his room on the second floor. When Forsyth followed him and knocked on the door, Allen shot through the door and killed him. He was arrested and placed in the Augusta jail. *The Augusta Chronicle* noted that he was "the once celebrated Methodist preacher, nearly six feet high, smooth speech under a thin cloak of sanctity, and about 40 years of age." Many in Elbert County took Allen's side, supported him, and proposed an insanity plea. Beverly, however, did not wait for a trial; he escaped from the Augusta jail and fled to his brother's house in Elbert County.

Robert Forsyth was the first federal law enforcement to be killed in the line of duty. The authorities felt they could not allow the deed to go unpunished, so they pursued Allen, rearrested him, and locked him temporarily in the Elbert County jail. But he was so popular among his homefolks that a mob of more than 200 angry Elbert County citizens stormed the jail and freed him. He fled to the Kentucky frontier, Logan County, and the law made no effort to follow. There he stayed, adopted the doctrine of Universalism, preached, and even practiced medicine until he died at the age of ninety in the mid-1840s.

Interestingly, the great Methodist minister, Peter Cartwright, was with him when he died. He had boarded with the Allen family when he was a boy. Allen told his friend that his crime of murder had been so bad that the mercy of God would not extend to him, and he warned his family and friends, as Cartwright put it, "not to come to that place of torment to which he found himself eternally damned." Over that half century, Beverly Allen had become a legend, a hero like Robin Hood whom the authorities were always after but could not catch. Beverly Allen's brother, William, had continued to be a highly respected businessman in Elbert County and lived in a community named Beverly.

Such was some of the family history of the beautiful and spirited Susan Beverly Allen with whom the young lawyer Young L. G. Harris was to fall in love and marry.

Harris and McIntosh, Elberton's two young lawyers, had the most impressive office building in town. Built around 1800, the rooms were more than twenty-five feet square with extremely high ceilings. Portions of the woodwork were solid mahogany brought to Savannah on sailing vessels and then over land to Elberton. Some years after the Civil War, this landmark was destroyed by fire. But for many years it was one of the great buildings in Elberton.

In 1840, the year Beverly Allen died in Kentucky, Young Harris was elected to the Georgia House of Representatives from Elbert County. He was twenty-eight years old.

Young L.G. Harris

It was a time of economic distress in Georgia caused by the panic of 1837. Cotton had dropped to four cents a pound and commerce in the state was stagnant. The state treasury was nearly empty and the state's credit was at an all-time low. Bold action was called for, and Governor Charles J. McDonald tried his best to meet the challenge. First, he convinced the legislature that the counties were not up to the job of collecting property taxes and that the state should collect them. He also advocated the repeal of the Common School Act that had been passed three years before to provide free schools for all. Harris opposed this repeal; he was a champion of education, and the law's author was State

Representative Alexander H. Stephens, one of Harris's personal friends. Governor McDonald also called for higher taxes and argued that the legislature should not receive their salaries until all state expenses had first been paid.

Harris admired McDonald as a man who would make hard decisions and helped him on most issues. The young attorney was captivated with the challenge of the legislative process, the give and take it took to search for the common ground that both sides could support. But he did not like living in Milledgeville. He thought the inns were dirty and the food below average. Too many hawkers and walkers and too much drinking went on, which bothered the teetotaler Harris. He also thought they charged too much to stable and feed his horse. That was one reason he enjoyed meeting Etheldred Swain from Emanuel County. For many years, Representative Swain, rather than pay for the care of a horse, just walked the sixty miles from his house to the capital. Swain also saved in other ways; he would not stay in a hotel but brought a bedroll, frying pan, rifle, and a tent that he pitched on the banks of nearby Fishing Creek. Known to often indulge in a little drink, Swain once took a shot at the eagle that had been painted on the front of the capitol. "Thought it was real," he explained. It did no damage to the building with its three-foot thick walls.

Some legislators who could afford it brought their wives to the capitol city, and Young decided that if and when he ever served in the legislature again, he would bring Susan. Traveling shows of all descriptions came to town during the legislative session. One featured a 700-pound polar bear and a 10-year-old mule the size of a dog. Trained horses were always a big hit as well as musicals. The first year Harris was there in 1841, a minstrel show performed in a large frame building to the east of Statehouse Square to a capacity audience. The climax of the show was the performers singing "Old Dan Tucker" with flailing banjos loudly filling the air. It was the first time the song had ever been heard in Milledgeville: "Old Dan Tucker was a fine ole man. He washed his face in a frying pan, combed his hair with a wagon wheel, died with a toothache in his heel. Old Dan Tucker, he got

drunk Fell in the fire, kicked up a chunk Red hot coals in his shoe
Laudamercy, how de ashes flew." And on and on and on . . . .

The audience stood and cheered, threw their hats in the air, and
stomped their feet so hard that the performance had to be temporarily
halted to prevent the collapse of the building. The performers had
never seen such a response and were surprised to learn that the
Reverend Dan Tucker was from up the state in Elbert County, which
Young Harris at that time represented.

Military balls were also popular and would be staged at the slight-
est provocation. But the most "highfalutin" or sophisticated,
depending on who was describing it, were the plays and candlelight
readings put on by the Milledgeville Thespian Society.

Even though the governor's residence had just been completed in
Milledgeville and a grand three-story hotel was on the way, there was
already talk of moving the seat of government away from Milledgeville
to another location. The city of Macon had many supporters as did
Atlanta. One of the things that made Milledgeville undesirable was
that the state penitentiary was located there, and when many of the
convicts were released, they remained in town. Some even built shacks
to live in on the capitol grounds. Also, often the families of the imprisoned would move to Milledgeville to be closer to their loved ones.

Harris particularly enjoyed meeting the representatives from some
of the new counties. Harris thought Johnson P. Wellborn of Union
County was impressive. A mountaineer through and through, he had
already served several terms, had been defeated by John Bryson, who
lived in Brasstown Valley, and then came back in 1841 to serve with
Young Harris.

A new county, Dade, had just been created three years before up
in the northwest corner of the state. It was coalmining country, and
Andrew Tuttle was the newly elected representative. Although Rabun
was not a new county, having been created in 1819, it was another
mountain county, and its representative, Horace Cannon, was one of
the legislature's most colorful members. Later, Harris would serve with
a John Quincy Adams from Rabun and would write Susan, "Well, I
met John Quincy Adams today, maybe Andrew Jackson tomorrow."

His legislative colleagues from neighboring Clarke County were Asbury Hall and two veteran legislators, Robert H. Moore and William Stroud. The two other representatives from Elbert were T. W. Rucker from one of the pioneer families and James Patterson. A few years later, one of Young's best friends, McAlpin A. Arnold, would represent Elbert, and Young would represent Clarke.

But of all the members, his personal favorite was Alexander H. Stephens, his not-too-distant neighbor from Crawfordville. "The best mind in the legislature," everyone agreed. He too was a strong supporter of education and was pleased when Harris joined him against Governor McDonald's desire to repeal his recently passed Common School legislation.

Harris visited Stephens on more than one occasion at his home, "Liberty Hall" in Crawfordville, where he lived with his brother Linton and his beloved dog "Rio." And Harris was devastated in 1883 when that feeble little body drew its last breath after serving as governor only 119 days. Harris would tell his friend and coworker, Colonel W. W. Thomas, "he should never have made that long trip to Savannah; he was too weak for that celebration even if it was Georgia's 150th birthday."

Harris also respected and worked closely with George Washington Towns, the handsome and courtly former congressman, when Towns was governor in 1847–1851. As a legislator from Clarke County at that time, he gave Towns his strong support on the completion of the Western and Atlantic Railroad and his plan for using tax revenue to support public schools. State aid was an ongoing issue at that time. Harris did think Towns went too far in 1850 when as governor he began to call for secession right after the Compromise of 1850.

Susan joined him when he came back to the legislature as a member from Clarke County. She loved living in Milledgeville with Young during the session and attending some of the festivities of the legislature. The reception at the executive mansion in December 1851 following the inauguration of Howell Cobb as governor was the most lavish party Milledgeville had ever seen. It was reported, "The display of beauty and fashion . . . would have graced the most stylish metropolitan entertainment . . . with pyramids of snowy cakes, spun candies, ice cream and blancmanges, turkeys, oysters, hams, salads, etc." But no liquor or wine because the wife of Howell Cobb would not allow it. It was not because Cobb was a frugal man. He once ordered 1,000 cigars from Savannah and charged them to the state. Cobb, also from Clarke County, was gregarious and charming and had served six terms in Congress before becoming governor. He had even been elected Speaker of the U.S. House of Representatives at the age of thirty-four, and it was he who had presided over the Compromise of 1850.

Cobb's wife, Mary Ann, was from Milledgeville and was a devout member of the local Baptist church. She hated the glitter of politics that so attracted her husband. Susan was disappointed to see that Mrs. Cobb would not appear in the receiving line with her husband. She could not imagine a wife doing that to a husband.

The opposite was true of the next first lady, Mrs. Herschel V. Johnson, the niece of former president James K. Polk. She was always the belle of the balls, sparkling and gracious while her husband was stern and unsociable. But Johnson was a scholarly and eloquent speaker as well as a skilled brick mason.

Living in Elbert County, Young Harris had everything an up-and-coming lawyer could have wanted. Everything, that is, except his independence. He felt much of his early success had come from being an Allen-in-law, and he desperately wanted to be his own man. So in the early 1840s he had moved out of the county dominated by his in-laws and moved back to Clarke County. Susan, ever the supportive wife, understood. She loved the city of Athens with its beautiful trees and tasteful architecture. She thought it was the social and cultural center of Georgia.

Young continued to practice law and be engaged in politics. Three times, in 1846, 1848, and 1850, he was elected to serve in the Georgia House of Representatives from Clarke County. He also served as city judge of Athens for several years, and most people came to refer to him as "Judge Harris." He was a distinguished-looking man, about six feet with an impressive bearing, solidly built with a salt and pepper mustache and goatee. More and more he turned his talents to business; he became a banker and was one of the organizers of the

Southern Mutual Life Insurance Company. It was incorporated in Macon and had its headquarters in Griffin, Georgia, until December 1848, when Harris used his influence to move it to Athens. A member of its board of directors from the beginning, Harris in 1866, right after the war, became its president. He had seen the need for a regional mutual company to provide insurance against fire for those outside the larger metropolitan areas. Up until then, insurance was only available for large investor-owned northern companies. Until his death nearly thirty years later in 1894, Harris devoted most of his time and talent to making the company a phenomenal success and himself a wealthy man.

Judge Harris and Susan were living in Clarke County when the Civil War began. The Judge had seen the war coming for sometime. He knew Lincoln was right that "a house divided against itself cannot stand." Slavery had split the country apart. The presidential election of 1860 split it even further. The Democratic Party, filled with dissension over the issue, held its national convention in Charleston, South Carolina, but immediately broke up over the issue of expanding slavery in the territories. Later the southern wing of the Democratic Party met and nominated John C. Breckinridge for president, and the main group nominated Stephen A. Douglas, senator from Illinois for president, and, surprisingly, Herschel V. Johnson of Georgia as vice president even though no one from Georgia was even there. The Republicans nominated Abraham Lincoln and, to add to the confusion, a new Constitutional Union Party nominated John Bell.

Lincoln was elected, followed by secession and war. Actual combat came no closer to Athens than Atlanta in 1864, and the first year ordinary life in Athens went on as usual. It would not continue; factories had to limit their manufacturing because raw materials and consumer goods began to be in short supply. In 1863 the university closed because students and some faculty went into home guard units. The poor suffered the most, as they always do, because the men in the family had gone to war and the mothers and children were left to struggle on their own. Athens also became a refugee city. Women, children and older men poured into the city from the war-torn South.

They lived in rented homes, hotel rooms and in the closed classrooms of the university.

Through all this Susan and the Judge did what they could to help the poor and needy. Young felt guilty that his younger brother-in-law and former law partner, William M. McIntosh, was out there in the thick of the war while he, now in his fifties, was in Athens. He was proud when he learned that William had made colonel in the 15th Georgia Infantry Confederate Army. McIntosh wrote the following letter to Harris in the first year of the war:

Dear Harris,

I received, a few days ago, your very kind letter. Amid my camp duties, I assure you, I think of you often, and certainly, would have written to you before this if I could have found anything of interest to communicate.

Although we are almost in the very face of the enemy we actually know less of what is transpiring around us than you do at home. We get almost all of our reliable information from the newspapers and you have better means of access to them than we have. We are expecting a fight shortly. Indeed, we have been looking for it for some time. We know nothing with certainty about our future movements. We are left to inference from facts which our commanding officers are forced to communicate to us. They have issued orders to all of the Brigades to keep constantly on hand three days cooked rations, and are, also moving all the sick to the rear. From these things we conclude that an advance movement is intended, but when it will be put into operation, we can form no definite opinion. . . . Our Regiment has suffered very much on account of the measles. It has been our greatest scourge. There are not now more than 450 of our men fit for duty. . . . So far as I am concerned, I have no reason to complain.

My friend, the greatest trouble I have had to encounter since I embarked in the defense of my country is the great distress of my wife. But, I am not disposed to complain. Thousands of others have gone through the same ordeal. I speak of this to show you place me under great obligations by expressing a willingness and desire to serve not only me, but those I have left behind. Yourself and Sister

Susan, I have no doubt, can do much to reconcile Lou, and she, as well as myself, will appreciate your kindness . . . .

I have given myself to the cause of my country. If we are to be enslaved I hope never to live to see it. If we are to achieve our independence, of course, I wish to live and enjoy the fruits. But many perils beset the soldier and if I never return I know without asking it that both you and Sister Susan would interest yourselves for those left behind who are dearer to me than life itself . . . .

Truly your friend,
W. M. McINTOSH.

He did not return. The following year, 1862, McIntosh was killed, and both the Judge and Susan grieved for weeks. "He was a warrior just like his ancestors," Harris said to a friend, thinking of Lachlan McIntosh, the Revolutionary hero who was with Washington at Valley Forge and who killed one of the signers of the Declaration of Independence, Button Gwinnett, in a duel.

Although Young Harris did not serve in the war, he was always a son of the South. After the war was over, he liked to tell the "worst and best" during one week of the conflict in Georgia. It seems that when Sherman was marching through Georgia in 1864 and got close to Milledgeville, he selected as his escort a Georgian from that area, a Lieutenant David Snelling, who had deserted the Confederate Army and gone over to the Union. Having lived in the Milledgeville area, Snelling seemed to take pleasure in settling some old grudges from the past by burning houses and barns and confiscating a thousand bushels of peanuts at Howell Cobb's Hurricane plantation.

This traitor galled Young Harris, and often he would fuss about it. But then in the same breath he enjoyed telling about the contrast to Snelling: a twenty-year-old also from the area named James Rufus Kelly. He had become a legend for heroic fighting in Virginia, where he had lost a leg, and had a disability discharge in his pocket, but he wouldn't quit fighting. Although on crutches when Sherman came through, Kelly and one other soldier delayed the capture of the town of Gordon, Georgia, near Milledgeville for more than an hour. Kelly was captured and sentenced to death but escaped and lived to teach school for more than fifty years in Wilkinson County. But when Snelling, Sherman's escort, came back to Georgia after the war, his life was threatened and he was run out of town. "He died somewhere up in the Ozarks," Harris recounted, never tiring of drawing the contrast between these two young Georgia soldiers.

Like Artemas Lester before him who started the school and never saw it, so it was with Judge Harris; the benefactor never got to see the results of his work. But he talked about the college everywhere he went throughout Georgia, particularly in the surrounding Athens area. Although the University of Georgia was there in all its glory, Judge Harris became a persistent recruiter in the Athens area for the little college up in the mountains that bore his name.

Typical were the trips he made to Danielsville, about twenty miles from Athens. He would drive his buggy, often alone, and would speak in the Methodist churches of Madison and Oglethorpe counties. Years earlier he had made friends with the Reverend Thomas J. Adams, a Methodist circuit rider who had settled on a small farm in that area. He had a lovely wife named Eliza whose mother had come to nearby Elbert County from Opelika, Alabama. They had six sons.

When Preacher Adams feared that he would not be able to send all those boys to college, he hit upon the idea of teaching them Munson's shorthand since stenographers were much in demand. That was the kind of thinking that had impressed Judge Harris. He understood the sorrow when Mrs. Adams died in 1892 just a few months after Judge Harris had visited in her home. He could not help thinking of the earlier loss of his dear Susan. Later, the Reverend Adams was to die one year after Judge Harris.

The Adams boys continued to manage the farm, perform the household chores, and look after the younger ones. In 1898, one of the boys, Emory Lovick, then eighteen, decided to go to Young Harris and see firsthand what Judge Harris had been so excited about. He borrowed money from his cousin to make the trip and then did odd jobs in the community as he attended college. After graduation, Lovick owed $161, so he went to Philadelphia to work for his older brother, Wilbur, who had gotten a job with the Coca-Cola Company. There Lovick looked after horses, cleaned up the offices, and slept in one of them. He lived on less than $8.00 a month, and within six months he had saved enough to pay the debt. Meanwhile, he had corresponded with the new president of Young Harris College, Dr. Joe Sharp, who had come to Young Harris when Adams was a student and knew the hardworking lad well. Dr. Sharp offered him room and board and $20.00 a month if he would come back and be a teacher. Although in Philadelphia he was making $50.00 a month and his brother offered him $75.00 if he'd stay, he did not even write Dr. Sharp back. He just packed his meager belongings and came back to Young Harris. He taught math, Latin, and Bible and preached in the local churches. In 1904, he married May Sanderson, the daughter of Nancy Louise, the woman who had helped Artemas and Reverend Edwards get the school started.

On April 28, 1894, at the age of eighty-two, Judge Harris went to his reward. Alert to the end, he died peacefully in his sleep after a brief illness. His alter ego, W. W. Thomas, was with him in his final hours and described his beloved friend this way:

> Conspicuous for his piety, beloved for his generosity, revered for his philanthropy, illustrious for his good deeds, admired always for his Christian graces and his domestic virtues, he was none the less honored for his high integrity, and gave to his vocation, with all this wealth of character, a lifetime of devotion and the highest business sagacity.

> Not tears nor grief befit the passing of a life so full, so noble and well rounded as that of our lamented associate and friend. His is that peace which passeth all understanding, and we know that he wears a crown in the light that never fails.

The *Athens Banner* carried this notice in bold print: "To the Pearly Gates the Spirit of the Noble and Great has fled: A Grand Old Hero of Christ's Army lays down his untarnished armor at the Master's feet: the Friend of the poor, a philanthropist without pride, he was indeed a pillar of the church, known and loved by all."

It is impossible to overestimate the contribution this man made to Young Harris College. Not just in money and tangible gifts but in the credibility his name gave it far beyond that beautiful valley. Bishop and Emory College president Atticus G. Haygood got it right when he said, "Young Harris College owes almost everything to one generous, consecrated Georgia Methodist."

But the Judge's weary old bones did not get to rest. Soon after his death, a lawsuit was brought contesting his will. Suing were some forty "heirs-at-law" on his deceased brother's side of the family. They maintained that the Judge had "monomania" about giving his fortune away to worthy causes, and his wife's relatives and they, "his poor relatives," should receive some of it. They specifically objected to one-third of the estate going to Emory and Young Harris College and the provision that specified his 400-acre plantation in Clarke County be sold and the proceeds divided equally between the Foreign Mission Society and the Church Extension Society of the Methodist Episcopal Church South. They also questioned his sanity, maintaining that he once said he saw his deceased wife Susan. in the front yard. The Judge himself had written the will, and Colonel W. W. Thomas was the executor. In June 1897 the Supreme Court of Georgia ruled in favor of the original will and against the "heirs-at-law." The Judge's "monomania" for good causes was validated.

One Sharp Man

Raw boned, he stood an erect 6'1" and weighed 180 pounds. He could plow a furrow straight as a string and had—hundreds of them. He could castrate a bull calf or a boar pig and had—dozens of them. No student—even the strongest—ever defeated him in arm wrestling. But this same man could also translate mythology from the original Greek and spoke Latin as if he had served in the Roman Senate. The man could preach sermons filled with fire and brimstone and sermons of such tenderness they made grown men weep. He was up like a shot when a female entered the room, and he always tipped his hat when he met a woman. Yet, this same man at a mixed dinner table after he had taken a mouthful of soup that was too hot, spit it on the floor with the casual explanation, "Now a fool would have swallowed that."

This man's name was Joe Sharp. He was from Waleska, a little crossroad settlement in upper Cherokee County, Georgia. The Lewis W. Reinhardt family, of German descent, moved there in 1832 from Gainesville to start a gristmill on Shoal Creek. "Warluskee" was an Indian princess who had once lived in that area, so they named their settlement in her honor. It was about seventy-five miles from Brasstown Valley.

In 1855, three Sharp brothers came there from Walhalla,

Joseph A. Sharp

South Carolina, near the Georgia line. They were John J. A. Sharp, White Sharp, and Joseph M. Sharp. They opened a store, a cotton gin, and a tobacco factory, and they farmed. Later, Joseph M. would be a teacher. The Civil War interrupted their lives, and they served in the Confederate Army. On March 30, 1864, Joseph M. became the father of Joseph Astor Sharp.

On that same day about seventy-five miles north in Chattanooga, a Union general, tall, fidgety, and red-haired was awaiting approval from his commander in Virginia, U. S. Grant. His name was William Tecumseh Sherman, and his plan was not just to capture Atlanta but to march his army of 100,000 men straight through Georgia to the Atlantic Ocean at Savannah. The most daring part of the plan, which Grant was pondering, was that Sherman wanted to operate without the conventional supply line. He argued he could feed this huge army by living off the land he was passing through.

Grant was unsure, and President Lincoln also questioned the wisdom of it. He could not afford a mistake in the summer of an election year. He also had some doubts about this man Sherman. A West Point graduate, yes, but one who loved to paint and had been a schoolmaster in Louisiana. One Northern paper had earlier called him "insane," and later, Sherman himself would write in his memoirs he knew that if he failed, it would be called "the wild notion of a crazy fool." But Grant, who had an uncanny ability to judge soldiers and evaluate military strategy, sat down on a log in Virginia in early May and with a pencil wrote a telegram that gave Sherman the orders to undertake this highly risky move.

So, like a runaway locomotive, down the Western and Atlantic Railroad came Sherman and his men. Tearing up the rails, they built huge bonfires, heated the middle of the rails red hot, and then twisted them into "Sherman's horseshoes," never to be used again.

It was a fight all the way. After a three-day battle at Resaca, Sherman moved on to Pumpkin Vine Creek and New Hope Church. Then came Kennesaw, and after bloody fighting, Atlanta was captured on September 2, 1864. This victory assured Lincoln would be reelected for a second term.

Sherman showed no mercy. He had said, "War is hell," and he was proving it. He believed that the worst one can make war, the quicker it would be over. He burned Atlanta and then divided his army into two lines: one going to Macon, the other to Milledgeville. His men destroyed everything in the sixty-mile path. It was estimated that 100 million dollars of property was taken or destroyed. Only one-fifth of that was actually used by the soldiers. "Total War," it was called. Two thousand miles of railroad were destroyed, and some of the soldiers held a mock session of the legislature at the capitol in Milledgeville where they "repealed" the secession law.

When Sherman took Savannah on December 21, 1864, after being in Georgia for almost eight months, he sent President Lincoln a telegram: "I beg to present to you as a Christmas present the City of Savannah." In less then five months, the war would be over. And that was what was going on in the first year of the life of Joe Sharp.

He grew up on a farm, the best young "hand" in the area. He was tall for his age, strong and tireless. His work ethic was the talk of the community. He was also a religious young man and attended the old Briarpatch Church with both Methodists and Baptists. Like most things in Waleska, it had been founded in 1834 by Lewis W. Reinhardt.

When Joe was twelve years old and Reconstruction had ended, Mr. Joseph M. Sharp turned to his true love; for not only was he a farmer and businessman, but he was also an educator, a natural at home in the classroom.

About two miles from Waleska was the first public school in that area called "Swayback." It had been started in 1873 with Miss Julie Crawford as the only teacher. Three years later, Mr. Sharp became its headmaster. Students attended from as far away as eight miles. They ranged in age from six to twenty years old. Young Joe took to school like a fish to water. He became a voracious reader; he loved the stories and poems and found that he could memorize easily.

In 1883, Joe's uncle, Colonel John J. A. Sharp, and his brother-in-law, Captain Augustus M. Reinhardt, built a classroom in Waleska. Later, Captain Reinhardt went to the North Georgia Conference of the Methodist Church and made an appeal for a "strong preacher and teacher" to come to Waleska and take charge of the school with a guarantee of 1,000 dollars a year. The Reverend James T. Linn was sent and opened the school in January 1884, but a cyclone came along only a few weeks later and destroyed the building. The school would not be ready again for occupancy until January 1885, about the same time Artemas Lester was to make his journey to Brasstown Valley.

In 1888, Joe Sharp, then twenty-four years old, was a member of Reinhardt's first graduating class, which included four others who had completed the necessary courses for the academy diplomas. He then went to Emory College and graduated in 1892 with a major in English literature. He was elected superintendent of Stilesboro High School and stayed in that position for two years. Feeling the call to preach, he joined the North Georgia Methodist Conference and was sent by that body as a preacher and teacher to Fairmount, the same location where the young Mark Edwards had been in the 1880s before going on to become the first principal and teacher at McTyeire Institute.

In 1899, the same thing happened to Joe Sharp. At the age of thirty-five, the Methodist Conference sent him to Young Harris College to become its president. It was truly a time when the man, the moment, and the institution met. As a new century was about to dawn, so was a new day for Young Harris College.

The school was then thirteen years old, and there had already been five different leaders placed in charge of it. They were all good, able, dedicated men, and each made important contributions to the future welfare of the school. Attendance, especially outside the mountain area, had been greater than anticipated. There were hundreds coming from far and wide and not just from Georgia. But the faculty was far too small. There were about 10 teachers for 400 students of all ages and grades from the fourth to four years of college. No president had ever been paid more than $750 a year, and usually he did not get that much because his salary came only after all the bills had been paid. Tuition was one dollar a month, and board was ten dollars a month. The outgo was greater than the income. The college would have died, merged, or moved to another location had it not been for the generosity and credibility of its namesake. And then the great benefactor died.

Young Harris College was in this situation when Joe Sharp became its president. He and his wife Ella, whom he always called "Sweet Apple," came in a buggy, a two-day trip from Fairmont. Here was a preacher, a teacher, a farmer, and an administrator with good business sense. Greatly gifted with a natural intelligence that enabled him to grasp subjects quicker than most, he often would ask a random student in chapel to recite any Bible verse, and then he would build a short sermon from it. But it was his strength of character that shone above everything else. Deeply religious, a man without vanity, he had indefinable magnetism and a sense of humor. He once asked one of the basketball players, "Are you drinking from the Fountain of Knowledge or just gargling?" In his mid-thirties he was in superb physical condition, still a lean, roughhewn farm boy with long arms and big, calloused hands with wrists so wide, Mrs. Sharp had to reset the buttons on the cuffs of his shirts. Sometimes he'd just leave them unbuttoned.

It was not surprising that one of the first things he did after assuming the presidency was buy the college a 250-acre farm. Ironically, it was the same acreage that Colonel Thomas had tried to buy from "Buck" Erwin in 1885 for the college campus. It was rich bottomland along Brasstown Creek where corn and wheat and vegetables could be grown in abundance. He created pastureland where dairy cows could graze and provide good fresh milk for college students to drink. Pigs were raised by the dozens, and chickens provided eggs and meat. In short order, it became a farm producing and self-supporting just like the one he had helped his father build many years before. Sharp and the Erwin family became close friends, and in 1904, one Erwin baby was named Joseph Sharp Erwin.

Those who did not have the money to attend college could work their way through. At least twenty-five boys worked all summer for their board and tuition for the school year. Girls worked in the kitchen canning fruits and vegetables and waited tables during the school year. They became a special group that took pride being a member of the "working gang." It was a badge of honor years after they had graduated. Truth be told, they were Joe Sharp's pets, and often he would work side by side with them, the trousers of his suit rolled up to his knees and his tie slung over his shoulder.

In June 1902, Mrs. Nancy Louise Haynes Stephens Sanderson Robertson died. The funeral was held in the Susan B. Harris Chapel on the land she had generously made available for the college six years earlier. President Sharp and Reverend Alfred Corn officiated, and a huge crowd paid their respects to this spirited and far-sighted woman who was responsible for the schools' exact location in the valley. In 1903 the two largest boarding houses for boys burned to the ground. But that didn't stop the farmer and the builder; Sharp bought 228 acres for 200 dollars. Then he did a strange thing, it would seem to some. He told one of his best professors, E. L. Adams who taught Bible and Latin, "I want you to go up there in the Kirby Cove and supervise the cutting and sawing

Nancy Louise Haynes Stephens Sanderson Robertson

of enough timber to build a new dormitory. We had to turn away 20 girls this year, and our enrollment is hitting 450; we could go over 500 if we had the room." So "Fessor" Adams took off his tie and white shirt and put on his work clothes, and Hamby Hall was soon built. He, like Sharp, was as much at home with manual labor as he was in the classroom.

One of the students in the 1908 class was T. Jack Lance from Choestoe. Sharp liked these "Choestoe boys," as he called them. They had the same characteristics that he and Adams had; they were scholars, as he put it, "with calloused hands." And he often said, "I like someone who's not afraid to break a sweat." A few years later in 1916, there were three such Choestoans who graduated: Charles Reid, Henry Duckworth, and his brother Lon. The first two would become justices on the Georgia Supreme Court, and Lon would become an insurance executive much like Judge Harris and also chairman of the Georgia Democratic Party.

The little community of Young Harris continued to grow. There were no paved roads, and there wouldn't be one until the mid-1920s, and it would only be nine feet wide. Kerosene lamps provided the light and fireplaces the heat. But just over a couple mountains, through Unicoi Gap and downstream from the headwaters of the Chattahoochee River and Spoil Cane Creek, timber and lumber was becoming a big business. Right after the turn of the century, a sawmilling center went up almost overnight. In 1912, the Gainesville and Northwestern Railroad stretched thirty-seven miles to the town called "Helen," named for the daughter of the man who owned the sawmill. In less than two decades, thousands of acres of virgin timber were stripped, sawed, and shipped to builders all over the country. Then the once shiny new tracks and the hundreds of jobs disappeared as the "lumber rush," like the "gold rush," passed into history. About this same time, oriental chestnut trees were introduced into North America. They carried a fungus that rapidly spread to Appalachia, completely wiping out the American chestnut within forty years and changing the Appalachian forest forever.

Down the hill from the college, a new store building had replaced the old one where the first classes taught by Mark Edwards had been held. In the early evening hours after the day's work was done, supper had been eaten, and the woman of the house was cleaning up and getting the children ready for bed, some of the town's menfolk would gather there to swap stories about the day's happenings. Someone designated it the "loafer's bench."

In the summer, it was outside on a bench, and in the winter nail kegs around a pot-bellied stove. Often—some faculty members said *too* often—Joe Sharp could be found in their midst. Laughing loudly at a story, he would be reminded of one himself, and around the circle it would go. The townspeople adored him for this quality. It made them feel like he was one of them. Professor Adams, who lived across the street from the store, also was usually present. Once when a state politician was referred to as "a favorite son," "Fessor Adams," who would later be a state legislator himself, broke up the crowd with the question, "Is that a complete sentence?"

Many of the stories revolved around the hunts, the fox chases, and arguments around whose dog or what breed was best. Sharp enjoyed telling about one of the local men, bragging how well his dog would obey him. "Watch," the man said as he gave the command. "Blue, come here!" The dog got up but went in the opposite direction toward the house. "Come here, Blue," he said, somewhat angered and disappointed the dog was not performing well in front of a stranger. As the dog proceeded to the house and found a resting place under the front porch, the man added more confidently, "Or get under the porch."

An entire evening could be spent arguing the merits of a good coon or possum dog. The hunters would be divided over Blue Tick and the Black and Tan breeds. One favorite tale often told involved Bill Dean, a regular Friday night foxhunter, and some of his friends. Usually four or five of them with their dogs would go out, often on a Friday night, find a good spot, build up a big bonfire, wait until the dogs found a track, and listen as they would go barking, or "making music" as some of them called it.

After a time, the dogs would make a different kind of bark, a little faster "yip, yip" or a "treed" bark when they had run the fox in a hole. While all this was going on, the hunters would sit around the campfire telling tales and often drinking a little corn liquor. One night when things were unusually slow and one old man had gotten a little too much from the jar, he dozed off and went to sleep. The man had lost part of his leg below the knee when a tree had fallen on him, and he wore an old-fashioned wooded peg leg. No one noticed, but while the man was asleep, his wooden leg got into the fire and most of it burned off. Suddenly, the dogs hit a trail pretty close by and began to bark. Everyone jumped up to listen and be ready to run when they barked "treed." The old man jumped up and, without his peg leg, fell down. He jumped up again, somewhat groggy, and fell down again. "Are you all right?" one of the hunters asked him in the semi-darkness around the fire. "Yeah," the boozy one answered, "but be careful; there's a helluva hole every other step."

Joe Sharp and the members of his "working gang" were unaware of it at the time, but less than 100 miles west near Rome, Georgia, a similar educational experiment was beginning. Martha Berry had been born into a life of wealth and privilege. She was a debutante who was educated by a private tutor and traveled extensively in Europe. Had she chosen, she could have lived the life of a society matron in the most fashionable circles of national society. But she opted to spend it instead by providing an educational opportunity for the poor children of Appalachia.

She had wanted to be a writer and had set up a study in the log cabin on her father's plantation. One Sunday afternoon, pondering possible subjects for her writing, she heard children's voices in the woods outside. Looking out, she saw three boys in ragged homespun overalls. She invited them in and gave each an apple. While they ate, she told them some Bible stories, and she was so impressed by their rapt attention that she questioned them about their lives. Learning there was no school for them to attend, she invited them back the next Sunday.

They not only returned but also brought more children with them and then even more the next time. Everyone would gather around Miss Berry and listen in almost worshipful silence as she taught them from the Bible. The crowds each Sunday grew so large that she moved the sessions into an old church in a nearby community known as Possum Trot. On weekdays, she began to drive her buggy into remote nearby communities. She then took some of her money and built a schoolhouse and asked some of her wealthy friends to help her. In 1902, she built a dormitory and opened a boys' school where they worked to pay their expenses. In 1907, 150 boys were earning their education there. Two years later a girls' division was opened, and in 1926 it became Berry College.

Sharp enjoyed keeping up with politics and followed the various campaigns at all levels. But being the shrewd administrator he was, he kept much of his political likes and dislikes to himself. He was pleased when the state legislature in 1914 named a county for Allen D. Candler. Not to be confused with Asa G. Candler, the pharmacist from Villa Rica who for $2,300 bought two-thirds interest in a concoction he sold in his drug store and in 1892 formed the Coca-Cola Company. No, this was Allen Candler, one of only two mountain men elected governor, the other being Joe Brown. Known as the "one-eyed plow boy of Pigeon Roost," Candler was from neighboring Lumpkin County and was serving as governor when Sharp become president of Young Harris. It was said the tobacco-chewing mountaineer used such rough language that it would "tear the teeth out of a sausage grinder." A conservative, he called himself an "old-fashioned Democrat" without ties to any "ring, clique or faction." Sharp liked the toughness and independence and once told a friend, "That man knows 'gee' from 'haw.'"

Another governor whom Sharp admired and invited to come to Young Harris to speak to the students was the unfortunate but courageous John M. Slaton. He was Georgia's only governor who had to be protected by the State Militia from being lynched by an irate mob. About the most meek and mild individual you'd ever see in politics, Slaton was propelled into international notoriety by the Leo Frank case.

He had served with distinction as both Speaker of the House and president of the Senate when Georgia's Progressive governor, Hoke Smith, went to the U.S. Senate and Slaton became acting governor. He then ran and was elected for a full term, but before his inauguration, a fourteen-year-old girl, Mary Phagan, was found raped and murdered in the basement of an Atlanta pencil factory. The manager of the plant was a Jew from New York named Leo Frank. He was charged with the crime, convicted, and sentenced to hang in a raucous trial that did not meet, many said, the test of impartial justice. In fact, the judge himself said Frank's "innocence had been proved to a mathematical certainty."

The U.S. Supreme Court upheld the conviction and verdict. An international furor ensued, and a national movement to save Frank arose. More than 10,000 Georgians signed a petition to Governor Slaton to spare Frank's life, and on June 20, 1915, two days before the scheduled date of execution and six days before the governor's term was to end, Slaton commuted the sentence to life imprisonment, stating he was not convinced that Frank's guilt had been proved.

A mob of more than 5,000 bent on hanging the governor and dynamiting his home were dispelled after much violence. For his next five days in office, the Slatons were guarded around the clock, and then when his term expired, they left the country for an around-the-world trip.

Passions did not cool, and on August 16 while the Slatons were still abroad, an armed band of twenty-five men seized Frank from the prison, drove him 175 miles across Georgia, and hanged him as near to Mary Phagan's grave in Marietta as they could get. Slaton did not venture into politics again for fifteen years. When he ran for the U.S. Senate in 1930, he lost every county in Georgia except one. The solicitor who convicted Frank, Hugh Dorsey, was elected governor in 1916.

On the national level, Joe Sharp was an admirer of another educator, the scholarly president of Princeton University and then governor of New Jersey, Woodrow Wilson. Sharp saw Wilson not just as a fellow educator but also a fellow Southerner. He had been born in Virginia and lived as a child in Augusta, Georgia, when his father was the pastor at First Presbyterian Church. After college, the young Wilson had opened a law office on Marietta Street in Atlanta and married a Rome, Georgia, girl. Two of his daughters were born in Hall County. But then Wilson went back to New Jersey and taught political science and became president of Princeton. From there he was elected governor in 1910 and president of the United States in 1912.

On the local and state level, without a doubt, Sharp's favorite politician was Mauney D. Collins of Choestoe, one of the descendants of the Union County pioneer Thompson Collins. He did not attend Young Harris; he had gone to Mercer, but Sharp often saw him in action and told many that he was the best natural politician he had ever seen. Collins had started out teaching eighty-one students in a one-room schoolhouse, and once he taught thirteen months in one school year. The school month then was twenty days, and in some places the school term was only two or three months, so beginning in July 1905, going from a school in one county to another in another county and teaching on Saturdays, Collins had taught thirteen months by July 1906.

Sharp delighted in telling the story of some political opponents threatening Collins that they would see that he would never teach or be elected in their county, to which he replied, "Do as you wish; I remember where I left my mule."

Only once did Sharp test whether a talented and popular educator like himself could be elected. The local Democratic Committee talked him into being their candidate for state representative. Towns County was split almost exactly fifty-fifty between Democrats and Republicans. Sharp was narrowly defeated. From then on he was content to watch others, like a slick-fielding and slick-talking second baseman who talked Sharp into allowing him to organize a college baseball team in 1913. He was a small kid from Arkansas named Eurith Dickinson Rivers, whose oratorical talent would pull him rapidly up Georgia's political ladder. Sharp would not live to see him elected governor in 1936. Sharp also encouraged one of his faculty members to run for the state senate and after he won allowed him to take off from his teaching duties to serve in Atlanta.

Sharp himself, most people would tell you, was an excellent communicator. No histrionics, no flailing of arms; he was more a talker than an orator. Nowhere was he better than teaching a Sunday school class. His eyes were penetrating and his expressions captivating. He was the kind of communicator one would enjoy having in one's living room. He could turn on the juice, stampede a crowd when the occasion called for it, but mostly it was your wise and caring uncle that you heard when Joe Sharp talked.

One of the greatest and most dynamic speakers of the time was George W. Truett, and it has already been related how as a young man, he enraptured the annual Baptist Convention in 1885 with his speech soliciting help for his school in Hiawassee. Only a year after Sharp became president, he had a similar moment at the North Georgia Methodist Conference in Atlanta. There he acknowledged the generosity of Judge Harris, that great Methodist from Athens whom many of the delegates had known well. He told of Artemas Lester's dream and how those seven students that first cold day met in an abandoned store building. And then, after he had drawn them into his web and painted a picture of what the school was and could be, he told them a true story of what had happened only a few weeks before. A farmer from back in the mountain who, like his father and his father's father, could not read nor write but knew the rewards of an education and its cost, had brought a bull out of one of the nearby hollows and tied it outside the bottom of the chapel where the president's office at that time was located. "See that air bull," he said, pointing to a well-fed animal with mud a foot up its legs. "I've brung it to you. I want his worth in education for my young'un."

You could have heard a pin drop, and then some appreciative chuckles and then a standing ovation from the admiring crowd of preachers and laymen who would never forget it. They would retell it, use it in their sermons, and never forget it. It was what that school in the mountains was all about. "If you have done it unto the least of these, my brother, you have done it unto me." If anything could be said about Joseph Astor Sharp, and much praiseworthy was said, one of his Choestoe students, Jack Lance, put it best: "He was the friend of the boy and girl who had no money."

He enjoyed preaching, and some of his best-known sermon titles were "The Prodigal Son," "Be Sure Your Sins Will Find You Out," "Repent and Be Baptized," and "Blessed Are They That Do Hunger and Thirst After Righteousness."

According to Jack Lance, that Choestoe student who would one day follow him as president, his best sermon was on the subject of sin, and the outline went as follows: "(1) There is pleasure in sin; (2) There is profit in sin; (3) There is power in sin; (4) There is death in sin." Lance continued, "He did not mince words. It sounded like John the Baptist, and students remembered that sermon long after it was preached."

He preached no longer than thirty minutes and led the singing himself. It was said he possessed a good strong voice and loved belting out "When the Roll Is Called Up Yonder." After Sunday night services, he would often linger for as much as an hour to lead the faculty members in the next Sunday school lesson. Sometimes the faculty members would want to discuss his sermon they had just heard. Students often stayed, and they were welcome to join in the discussion.

A champion debate in 1908 had as its subject "Resolved that the teachings of Jesus were stronger proofs of His Divinity, than were His miracles." The Phi Chis had the affirmative that year and won the decision. Champion debates between the two debating societies, the Young Harris Debating Society and the Phi Chi Debating Society, were huge. Held at the end of the school year, usually the Friday night before commencement, in the Susan B. Harris Chapel, they attracted crowds that overflowed the building and spilled outside by the hundreds.

In 1916, after receiving an honorary doctorate from the University of Georgia, President Sharp decided he wanted to preach for a while and accepted an assignment to a downtown Atlanta church, Wesley Memorial. The farm boy was not comfortable in the city and the following year went to Oxford as head of the academy there.

But the mountain school was never far from his thoughts; it was lodged in his heart. One day in 1921 while playing rook with a couple of former YIIC professors who had followed him there, he announced, "I think they want me to go back to Young Harris. Would you go back with me?" They folded their cards and got ready to go back. He would be president for eight more glorious years before his death on March 27, 1930.

CHAPTER 15

The Sermon

A few days before Thanksgiving, back in 1885, thirty-four persons, including some from his other churches, had attended the service at the Zion Methodist church to bid their pastor farewell and hear the Reverend Artemas Lester's last sermon in Brasstown Valley.

"A man's heart plans his way, but the Lord directs his steps," that's what Solomon wrote in Proverbs 16:9, and that's my text for my last sermon in Brasstown Valley. "The Lord directs his steps." And because the Lord is directing our steps, we are going to do something in this valley that will be so unbelievable that a hundred years from now men will look at this school and say, human beings alone could not have done this. It took the Almighty; it took a miracle; it took a manifestation of God's power. I want them to understand that is the only way this school could be here. Goethe wrote, "An event which creates faith, that is the purpose of miracles." This school can and, I have faith, will be such an occurrence.

This school must not be some fleeting dream here today and gone tomorrow. And we must never forget that all things are possible with God. Repeat that with me: "All things are possible with God. Nothing is impossible with God."

The Bible is a book of miracles. From Genesis to Revelation. Angelic intervention, divine direction, it's all there. It is also a book on how to create your own miracle with God's help. It starts with faith. Never forget, my friends, that faith is the hinge on which miracles swing. Saint Augustine said miracles lead us to faith, and here's a good example. Remember Abraham and Sarah, two very old people, long past their childbearing years. And yet God chose them with Isaac to birth a nation. Surely with faith, this valley in these old mountains can birth a school.

But do we have that faith? Old Abraham struggled with what God had laid upon him. It tested his faith. But strength comes from struggle. We all know that, don't we?

We know adversity can make us stronger. Remember Sarah, she thought she was too old to bear children, so what did she do? She offered her handmaiden to Abraham, and he thought that would be an easier way to have a son and fulfill God's requirement. So Ishmael, the son of Abraham and Hagar, came from that lack of faith. But even though Abraham made that mistake, he learned from it and he didn't cancel the covenant he had made with God. He held fast to God's promise. And after many years Isaac was born. And then you remember, God tested Abraham again by telling him to offer Isaac as a sacrifice, a burnt offering. So again, Abraham, having faith in God, placed this long-awaited son on the altar, ready to kill him. Is there any wonder that Abraham has been called the Father of Faith?

You see, God's promise is to provide, but his requirement is that we make ourselves ready to receive. He doesn't always tell us the plan. We have to respond; then He reveals. He wants to know if our heart is right. That if we do this, He will do that. That's a great trade isn't it, our "this" for God's "that."

You remember young Isaac wanted to know why his father was gathering wood. He asked him, "Where is the lamb for the offering?" And you remember when Abraham was just about to plunge the knife and kill his own son, the angel of the Lord appeared, and Abraham heard the words, "Now I know you will not hold anything back from me. Let your son go and I will fulfill my promise to you to raise up a nation through him."

Sometimes our dreams are killed because we listen too much to naysayers. I've heard from some and I know you have. But when God is on our side, He can make a way when it seems there is no way. Didn't God show Moses and the Israelites how He could divide the Red Sea and then crash it down on the Egyptians? You know how God could do that? Because, in the first place, God had made the Red Sea. Surely He could make His sea obey His will. Never doubt it, my friends. God will part a sea for us when we need it. He may already have and we didn't even know it. Because we are the apple of His eye, we are the sheep of His pasture. Moses cried to God, "Show me your glory." That must be our cry. And He will answer.

Remember the miracle of feeding the 5,000. A little boy who had brought his little lunch, with the Master's help, ended up feeding the multitudes. That little boy was willing to give Jesus all he had, some barley loaves and a few fish, and because he did multitudes were fed. This little school I've asked you to help me start will feed multitudes in the years to come also because "little" becomes "much" when placed in the Master's hands. In the Old Testament Elisha fed 100 men with 20 loaves, but Christ fed 5,000 with five loaves. We cannot understand all this because we see through a glass darkly. Job explained it well: "Lo, He is strong."

I wish I had the eloquence of George Whitefield. He sometimes spoke to crowds of 25,000 and once in Glasgow, Scotland, he spoke to 100,000. He converted 10,000 sinners in that meeting. Me? I'll be doing good if I speak to a combined 10,000 in my lifetime. I haven't even reached the first thousand yet. Whitefield came to Georgia you know—just like John and Charles Wesley. He came across the Atlantic thirteen times, came to Savannah in the spring of 1738. Organized an orphanage, called it "Bethesda," which means "house of mercy." He'd had it tough as a boy himself. His daddy owned a tavern and he scrubbed floors. He wanted to help the little children of those first Georgia settlers who had died and left little orphans. He got a grant of 500 acres, said he wanted it to be a "house of mercy for many souls." I haven't been able to get one acre, but out of the goodness of her soul, Mrs. Sanderson got us two rooms with a roof over them.

I don't have Whitefield's persuasion. I wish I did. You know once he went to Philadelphia to raise money and Ben Franklin came to hear him. Later, Franklin, in his famous autobiography, wrote "I happened to attend one of his sermons. I perceived early he meant to take up a collection. I silently resolved he would get nothing from me. I had in my pocket a handful of copper money, three or four silver dollars and five pistoles of gold. As the sermon progressed, I began to soften and concluded to give the copper. Another stroke of oratory made me ashamed and determined me to give my silver; and he finished so admirably that I emptied my pockets into the collection dish, gold and all." That's how persuasive Whitefield was. I wish I could preach like that.

You know what my most fervent prayer is? My most fervent prayer is that someday a good Christian man, maybe a Methodist with a fat pocketbook and a big heart, will, like Mr. Franklin, empty his pockets into the collection dish for this school. I had hoped it would happen while I was here in the valley with you. But it didn't. But it will; just you wait and see. Because God works in miraculous ways, His wonders to behold. And someday a learned and wise man also like Ben Franklin, who could do so many things well, will become the head of this school, and he will send graduates to churches and state houses and judicial benches and halls of congress. There will be authors, entertainers, and famous poets come from this school. It's going to be like throwing a rock into a pond; the ripples will just keep going out.

How will that happen in this isolated and faraway valley, you ask? My friends, if an angel can find not only the prison that Peter was in but the very cell where Peter was locked up, an angel can find Brasstown Valley, believe me. And you know why? Because the Bible tells us prayer was made without ceasing. After Herod killed James and had Peter thrown in prison, it seemed a desperate situation. But Peter's fellow disciples had seen Jesus walk on water and calm the storm. They had hope and they prayed without ceasing. And yet, when Peter made that jail break, even those praying could hardly believe it when their prayers were answered. They—even the disciples—lacked the faith. We should never be surprised when God's angelic messenger intervenes, never. According to Hebrews 1:14, that is the purpose of angels. I believe in angels. I believe in demons. I believe in Satan and I believe in a living God.

Just as Paul did. His conversion on that road to Damascus was one of the great miracles of the Bible. He had been a persecutor of the church, he had consented to the stoning to death of Stephen, and this, it seems, preyed on his mind. This is how Doctor Luke, one of Paul's most constant companions, tells this story in Acts. Now, there are two other versions of this in the Bible, but I like this one because it's the one Paul told Luke so Luke got it firsthand.

And as he journeyed, he came near Damascus: and suddenly there shined round about him a light from heaven. And he fell to the earth; and heard a voice saying unto him, "Saul, Saul why persecutest thou me?"

And he said, "Who art thou, Lord?"

And the Lord said, "I am Jesus whom thou persecutest; it is hard for thee to kick against the pricks."

And he trembling and astonished said, "Lord, what wilt thou have me to do?" And the Lord said unto him, "Arise, and go into the city, and it shall be told thee what thou must do."

And the men which journeyed with him stood speechless, hearing a voice, but seeing no man.

And Saul arose from the earth and when his eyes were opened, he saw no man: but they led him by the hand, and brought him into Damascus. And he was three days without sight, and neither did eat nor drink.

And there was a certain disciple at Damascus, named Ananias, and the Lord said unto him, "Arise, and go into the street which is called Straight, and inquire in the house of Judas for *one* called Saul, of Tarsus: for behold, he prayeth, and hath seen in a vision a man named Ananias coming in, and putting his hand on him, that he might receive his sight."

Then Ananias answered, "Lord, we have heard by many of this man, how much evil he hath done to thy saints around Jerusalem. And here he hath authority from the chief priests to bind all that call on thy name."

But the Lord said unto him, "Go thy way: for he is a chosen vessel unto me, to bear my name before the Gentiles, and kings, and the children of Israel: For I will show him how great things he must suffer for my name's sake."

And for thirty years, Paul labored, suffering all kinds of hardships and danger until the Roman emperor Nero had him beheaded about 66 AD.

Not only was he miraculously converted himself, but Paul had the gift of prophecy and the power to work miracles. Truly Paul was a "chosen vessel" of the Lord. But, my friends, we can all be vessels of the Lord if we allow ourselves to be. I believe I was a chosen vessel to come to this beautiful valley for the specific reason of starting a school. I told this to the Reverend Hamby that night I gave myself unequivocally to the Lord. And immediately he asked me if I had studied the miracles of the Lord, the miracles of the Bible. I'll never forget it. His question took me by surprise and I stuttered and stammered like I'm prone to do sometimes. I mentioned some of the best known, the best I could, but since that night over two years ago I have thought and read—even listed on a sheet of paper the major and the minor ones. I have also come to believe many had occurred that did not make the Good Book. And many have occurred since it was written.

First, just what is a miracle? The best definition I have run into is that it is "a work wrought by a divine power for a divine purpose by means beyond the reach of man." In the Bible the miracles seem to come at critical moments, and there are at least 200 of them. In the New Testament they are used to validate Jesus' mission. You see, the Bible has miracles and it has parables. And it has been said that "miracles are parables of grace and parables are miracles of power." Now I'm not sure I understand that exactly but I'm working on it and you should too.

One type of miracle is God's power over nature like the Red Sea or turning water into wine. Another is God's power over disease like leprosy, blindness, lameness. Then power over death of which there are many examples, and, of course, power over demons. Many of the Old Testament miracles created the world, created these mountains, and, yes, created this valley. Others destroyed God's enemies. In the New Testament they largely confirm that Jesus Christ is God manifest in flesh. There is also the miracle of God's abiding power. The years do not lessen His authority. It is the same today as it was 10,000 years ago. Nothing can destroy it. Miracles of his divine wisdom are seen every second of the day, every day of the week, every week of the month, every month of the year, every year of the century, every century of the millennium. Every time the day breaks, every time a bird sings, every time a baby coos, those are miracles great and marvelous in God's universe. Say Amen!

As one reads the Bible, it is clear that miracles are not limited to just one class of people. Every believer of Jesus Christ can tap into His power in the moment of need with the power of prayer. "If thou shalt confess with the mouth the Lord Jesus and shalt believe in thine heart that God has raised Him from the dead, thou shalt be saved," Paul tells us in Romans 10:9. "So I will glory in reproaches and in persecutions, in distresses for Christ sake, for when I am weak, then am I strong," he says in 2 Corinthians 12:10. So we must be, as James tells us, "doers of the word and not hearers only."

I wish I had the use of words like Charles Wesley. No one has described the miracles of the virgin birth and the miracles of the resurrection like that "Sweet Singer of Methodism." He wrote "Hark the Herald Angels Sing" about the first and "Christ the Lord Is Risen Today" about the latter. He wrote both just a few years after he returned to England from Georgia and about a year after his conversion. He didn't call them "angels" in his original version, but the old English "welkin," which means "vault of heaven." The music was added about a hundred years later. You'll be singing it soon. Christmas will be here before you know it. My favorite phrases are "Glory to the newborn King" and, what I believe are the most powerful four words ever written to describe the reason Christ was born, "God and sinners reconciled." Isn't that what it's all about?

And then that great Easter hymn, "Christ the Lord Is Risen Today," that captures the joy of our Lord's resurrection and the ecstasy it brings to the believer to know that all followers of Christ will conquer death as did our Master. The "alleluias" were not in the original. They were added later. Alleluia means "Praise the Lord." Say "Alleluia," church!

And, of course, Wesley wrote "O for a Thousand Tongues to Sing," and that is going to be our closing hymn in a few minutes. He got the idea for that song from a Moravian friend, Peter Bohler, who once said in a sermon, "Had I a thousand tongues, I would praise Him with all of them." And I like "Soldiers of Christ arise and put your armor on." You see, it took great courage to do what the early

Methodists did. And I've always carried around with me Wesley's tender haunting words "Depth of mercy! Can there be mercy still reserved for me? Can my God, His wrath forbear, me the chief of sinners, spare?"

And "A Charge to Keep I Have," based on the book of Leviticus where Moses says to Aaron and his sons, "Therefore, shall ye abide at the door of the tabernacle of the congregation day and night seven days and keep the charge of the Lord." That's what we are doing with this school: Keeping the charge of the Lord. I believe that with all my heart. And I want you to believe it too. This school will be our charge to keep!

And the great hymn emphasizing how the love of Jesus and God's grace can make the sinner whole, "Jesus, Lover of My Soul." Henry Ward Beecher, a great writer himself, wrote that he had rather to have written that song, as he put it, "than to have the fame of all the kings who have served on this earth." There's a true story from the Civil War about this hymn. A Confederate soldier named Levi Hefner was sent out one night by his commanding officer, Robert E. Lee, to take a message through an area partially occupied by Union troops. As he approached a bridge, his horse bolted and reared nervously. He dismounted and attempted to calm him. In the darkness, Hefner began singing softly this old familiar hymn, "Jesus, Lover of My Soul." In a few minutes the horse became quiet. Hefner mounted him, crossed the bridge without incident, and completed his mission.

Years after the war, Hefner attended a reunion of soldiers from both sides. They gathered in small groups to share experiences they remembered from the war. A Union soldier from Ohio remembered standing guard one dark night at a bridge. He had been ordered to shoot anyone approaching from the other side. During the night, he remembered, only one rider came his way, and he raised his rifle to shoot as soon as he could see the form in the darkness. The horse bolted, however, and the rider dismounted. To calm the horse, the rider began singing softly an old hymn, "Jesus, Lover of My Soul." The Union soldier was so touched, he said, that he let him pass by. You can imagine his amazement when Hefner told him he was that soldier. Now, wasn't that a miracle? I think so.

"Songs are so important," Thomas Carlyle once said. "Let me make a nation's songs and I care not who makes its laws." I believe that. Charles wrote over 6,500 hymns and poems in his lifetime. He composed many of them on horseback. It's a good time for thinking. I know just from the short time I've spent in the saddle. Sometimes he would be without something to write on and would come bursting into the house shouting "pen and ink, pen and ink." Then he would sit down and write out what he had been composing in his mind before he forgot it.

Charles Wesley kept up his hymn writing until the very last. As he lay dying, too feeble to use a pen, he called his wife to his bedside and dictated,

In age a feebleness extreme,
who shall a sinful worm redeem?
Jesus! My only hope thou art.
Strength of my flesh and heart,
Oh! Could I catch a smile from Thee,
and drop into eternity.

His daughter Sarah later indicated in a letter that he then grew passive, patient, and prostrate until life ebbed out.

A memorial tablet on the walls of the City Road Chapel in London where he is buried has first a favorite quotation of Charles: "God buries His workman but carries on His work." God will help you carry on the work of this school long after I'm gone. And He will help others carry on His work after you're gone.

And then there's the remarkable John Wesley, Charles older brother by three years, "the father of Methodism." A man who arose at four in the morning and preached several times daily for fifty years. At the age of eighty, he regretted he could only preach twice a day. He road 280,000 miles on horseback and preached 42,000 sermons. He also wrote hymns and books and pamphlets, biblical commentaries, and edited a fifty-volume series called *A Christian Library*. He also wrote in his journal every day. He believed a Christian life was a disciplined life, and he gave detailed instructions on everything under the sun. He published English, French, Latin, Greek, and Hebrew grammars. He wrote a book on child rearing that advocated "tough love" and boasted that no baby in his family was heard to cry out loud after they were a year old.

He and Charles came from a strong and big family who profoundly influenced his character and career. A strong mother named Susannah who did not hesitate to give her opinions on just about everything. His father was an Anglican minister and they had nineteen children.

John Wesley was thin and only 5'5", but he was tireless and filled with energy from the time he was a child. As a student at Oxford he started what he called a "Holy Club." This was where he and Charles first got to know George Whitefield. And this is where they first thought about going to the newest colony of Georgia. That turned out to be a bad experience for both of them. First, there was a terrible storm that almost destroyed the ship they were on. There were also some German Moravians on board, and while everyone else was scared to death they were calm and sang songs. That strong faith made a lasting impression on the Wesley brothers. Charles became secretary to General Oglethorpe, but they didn't get along and Charles became very unhappy. Oglethorpe took him out into the wilderness with him, even down to Frederica where he was building fortifications against the Spanish down in Florida. The general was worried that the Spanish would move northward against the English colonies. And he was right; they did try in 1742 and were turned back by the Georgians at the Battle of Bloody Marsh.

Both Wesleys were long gone back to England by then. Charles left after six months when Oglethorpe wouldn't even give him a cot to sleep on; John followed on December 21, 1737, and wrote, "I shook the dust of Georgia off my feet and left, having preached the gospel there not as long as I ought, but as long as I was able for one year and nine months." On the ship back home, he explained it this way: "I went to Georgia to convert souls and lo, I was not converted myself."

Back in England in May 1738, Charles had his experience of assurance and conversion, and three days later at a small religious society meeting on Aldersgate Street, John, as he put it, "felt my heart strangely warmed." They both were then free from doubt and sin. They had a clear sense of salvation with the faith that goes with it. John had worried about being "an almost Christian." Do you ever worry about that? After the Aldersgate experience, he never worried about that again. He went on to do the many great things we remember him for. As he brought about a great revival of Christianity in Great Britain. Historians today agree that his efforts saved England from the horrors of the French Revolution. But it was not easy; once a group in Wednesbury complained that Methodists sing psalms all day and make folk rise at five o'clock in the morning.

"I didn't mean to get so much into a history lesson, but this is my last time with you and I wanted to impress upon you how *great* things can come from *small* beginnings. With God's help, that's what will happen here. This is going to be *your* school. Not mine, but yours. The Methodist church's school, and I pray the church will draw it close to their bosom and support it. I pray generous benefactors will be found. And great leaders to lead it. And that God will look favorably upon it. It can be the turning point in a lot of lives. Perhaps lives will be "strangely warmed" on its campus over the years.

I started talking about miracles at the beginning of this message. In addition to miracles, I believe God at times also gives visions and dreams to guide and direct. God put Peter in Joppa so he would be nearby when God was ready for the gospel to be spread to the Gentiles in Caesarea just thirty miles away. He put me here to do what little I have done, and he will put someone else here to carry on and then someone else and someone else. I believe God can create a miracle here, not all at once but a little at a time. I believe it will be years before we truly can understand and appreciate and glorify what will be done in this valley.

I've never seen a turtle on a fencepost, have you? But if I did, or if you did, we'd know one thing: it did not get there by itself. Someone put it there. Someone had to put this school where it is. Someone else—many someones—will have to put it where it ultimately will be many years from now. For sure, it won't get there by itself. Just like that turtle on a fencepost.

If Christ sent you not forth, you go on a fool's errand. Christ sent me forth. I believe that deep in my soul. I am not here on a fool's errand. And neither are you. I prayed that God would make me a preacher. He had less to work with in me than you do with this school. My friends, I have no longing eye for big churches and fat salaries. I am just thankful to be a preacher of the glorious gospel of Jesus Christ. The power of a praying church is a mighty thing. In Matthew 18:20 Jesus promises that "when two or three are gathered together in my name, there am I in the midst of them." "In my name" is the key. That is the key to the future of this school. Thank you for the goodness you have shown me. I will never forget you.

Let us pray. I thank thee for these friends, dear Lord, for this Brasstown Valley and all whose lives have touched this servant in such a gentle and generous way. If I've been too pushy, I'm sorry, but ever since I came through Rock Gap I could see the sand going through the hourglass. Be with the next pastor and teacher, help him carry on the work that I've tried to start. Be with the families as they decide what is best for their children. And be with the teachers and leaders who will guide them. We do not know what the future holds but, dear God, we know who holds the future. And it is into your merciful hands we gladly place our future as well as the future of this church and this school. Amen.

My dear friends, I do not know whether I shall ever return to this place of indescribable beauty, but I will never forget the warm feeling I experienced upon entering into the presence of Brasstown Valley. However, it is the vision I behold for the school's future that permits me to leave with unspeakable joy and adulation. Now, commending all of you to the Keeper of Our Souls, I bid you an affectionate farewell.

Afterword

The North Georgia Conference relocated *Artemas Lester* eleven times in eighteen years, 1884–1902. He then transferred to the South Georgia Conference and had eleven more assignments in the next eighteen years. The largest city in which he served was Rome, where he was sent the year after Brasstown Valley. There he met and married Minnie W. Jack, whose father had been editor of a Rome newspaper. They had four children, including three sons who served in World War I. The oldest, Louis Marvin, worked with State School Superintendent M. D. Collins in the Georgia Department of Education. In 1892 while Artemas was assigned to Whitesburg, he started another educational venture, Hutcheson Institute, which lasted well into the 1900s.

Artemas Lester

After twenty-two ministries in thirty-six years, Artemas retired in 1920 and lived in College Park until his death on March 20, 1934. Mrs. Lester survived another twenty years. Her husband's headstone in the College Park Cemetery is marked only with "Rev. Artemas Lester" and the dates. Always well read, Artemas left a personal library that included an eleven-volume *Cyclopedia of Biblical, Theological and Ecclesiastical Literature*, many books by evangelists and foreign missionaries, a *History of Cyrus and Alexander*, and Plutarch's *Lives of Illustrious Men*. His Bible was so worn and laden with pencil marks that his son had it rebound to preserve it.

The only fragment of his handwriting, according to his grandson, the late Dr. William M. Lester, was on the last page of a letter to his son, Marvin, in France, 1918. It was written from Jakin, Georgia, another tiny speck on the map about the size of Young Harris. It ends in Artemas's bold and flowing script: "The Shield of Heaven be Always around you, Devotedly, Papa."

Artemas Lester never traveled outside of Georgia unless he veered over into the edge of North Carolina a few miles from Brasstown Valley. He never owned a car; he never owned a radio. "It was a simple life," his grandson wrote in a 1980 letter, "from youth to age."

When *Doctor Joseph A. Sharp* returned to Young Harris College in 1922, he assembled a top-flight faculty and continued to teach. This began some of the finest years in the history of the college. Charles R. Clegg was a graduate in 1927 and would become president in 1950. Dr. Sharp, who had hours of Shakespeare committed to memory, played Hamlet in an unforgettable performance one year. He bought a farm in Gordon County, hunted and fished, read voraciously, and owned the first automobile ever to come into Young Harris. He stayed close to the students, still put in workdays with his britches legs rolled up at the college farm, and he and Mrs. Sharp ate their meals in the dining hall. He inspired men like Scott B. Appleby, Willis Dobbs, W. T. Hamby, William Lawson Peel, J. C. Pruitt, Charles Reid, Charles Winship, and others to make significant financial contributions to the college.

Always in good health, he hardly ever got sick. But in 1929 he became ill and stayed that way through the winter and into the new year. In the spring of 1930, he had to be taken to the hospital and died on March 27 of that year. When he realized the end was drawing near and after being in a coma for sometime, he suddenly raised up and exclaimed triumphantly, "I've won! I've won for a million years! Thank God, I've won!" His eyelids closed and he rested on his pillow in calm and peace. After his death, many wanted to recognize this great man with a suitable monument. Some wanted a statue on the campus, and there were other suggestions. After several years, it was decided that the most appropriate way to memorialize this unique individual was to build a Methodist church and name it "Sharp Memorial," where the student body, faculty, and community could come to worship. It was completed and dedicated in 1949. The first hymn sung by the congregation at the church's opening was Charles Wesley's "O for a Thousand Tongues to Sing."

Reverend Marcus Hale Edwards left Young Harris at the end of 1887. He went on to pastor nine churches, including Monroe, Lawrenceville, Woodstock, and Clarkesville. In 1889, while he was packing to go to his next assignment in Mountville, he was stricken with paralysis. Unable to get up, he was helpless until his death six months later. Edwards was a faithful itinerant preacher for twenty years. History does not give him enough credit for the work he did those crucial first two years of the school's existence.

Reverend Charles C. Spence obtained a charter and opened the J. S. Green Institute in 1897 in Demorest, Georgia. In its first year it had 367 students from first grade to college juniors, but in two years it was beset by financial difficulties. The support that it expected to receive from the Methodist Church was not forthcoming. Reverend Spence cashed in his own life insurance policy to keep the school going and turned to the Congregationalist churches for help. In 1901, the American Missionary Board of the Congregationalist Church took the school under its wing, and in 1903 it became Piedmont College. Demorest is the hometown of baseball hall of famer Johnny Mize, and there is a Mize Center at the college. In 1995, Piedmont opened a campus in Athens, Georgia. In his will, Judge Harris left his gold watch and "cuff buttons" to Reverend Spence.

George W. Truett graduated from Baylor University in 1897 while pastoring the East Waco Baptist Church. After graduation he became the pastor of First Baptist Church in Dallas, Texas. He was there for more than 40 years, and the church grew from 800 members to 8,000. He was elected three times president of the Southern Baptist World Alliance. One of the world's great preachers for four decades, he died in 1944 at age seventy-seven. His homeplace in Hayesville, North Carolina, is open to the public as a convention center.

Reverend F. C. "Ferd" McConnell, who worked with George W. Truett in organizing the Hiawassee Academy, served as pastor at First Baptist Church in Gainesville; First Baptist Church in Lynchburg, Virginia; Calvary Baptist in Kansas City, Missouri; and First Baptist in Waco, Texas; and ended his career at Druid Hills Baptist in Atlanta. He also served as secretary of the Home Mission Board and was a trustee of Mercer University in Macon. For more than a quarter of a century, he returned each summer to Hiawassee to preach before the home folks. The magnificent church in Hiawassee and Truett-McConnell College in Cleveland, Georgia, are named in his honor and memory.

Sam P. Jones, a native of Alabama, lived in Cartersville, Georgia, and for many years was the agent for the Methodist Orphans Home. He first was a successful attorney but a drunkard. When his father was dying, Sam, then twenty-four, promised him he would give up drinking and become a Christian. He became one of the great evangelists of that time. At one revival in Nashville, Tennessee, he preached to 5,000 people three times a day and saw 10,000 converted. As could be expected, he often preached on temperance and the evils of alcohol. He was only fifty-nine when he died in 1906 while serving as a member of the Board of Trustees of Young Harris College.

Mitch and Narcissis Coker, who befriended Artemas that first night he was in the valley and gave him food and shelter often during the year, lived on the hillside of what is today Brasstown Valley Resort, about where the Twiggs Lookout is located. Their descendants still play important roles in the affairs of the community. Mrs. Hazel Coker Nichols is a retired teacher who has served on the Young Harris City Council for many years. A bridge across Corn Creek near Cupid's Falls is named in her honor. She was the one who confirmed the story of the mother cat and kittens under Artemas's bed his first night in the valley. Her aunt, Willie Coker Ross, and her husband, "Zeke" Ross, were fixtures in the town for years. Zeke served as mayor and Willie started the Old Union Cemetery Perpetual Care Fund. Their son, William, married Jane Miller and served on the council. Danny Nichols, the current mayor, is the great-grandson of Mitch and Narcissis.

John Bryson's descendants in the valley are fewer than they once were, but still they are many and prominent. The oldest is Hoyle Bryson, the uncle of the author. Now ninety-three and still sharp as a tack, he has lived in his house on Miller Street for almost seventy years. He fox-hunted with Bill Dean's sons and was a star athlete at YHC when Dr. Sharp was president. His deceased niece, June Bryson

Rushton, was the wife of Luke Rushton, the highly successful basketball coach at YHC for many years.

Bill Dean married Kitty Bryson three years after he told Artemas he had his eye on her. Unfortunately, Kitty died two years later, leaving an infant son. Bill later married Callie Christopher, a schoolteacher. He accumulated a lot of land, including much of the old Bryson property. He gave the college 100 acres in Kirby Cove. He and Callie had five children. One, Jim, became that lawyer Bill had told Artemas he wanted. Another son, Kiser, was a state representative and senator. Bill built his dream home, which no longer stands, at the end of Dean Street in Young Harris. When Bill died in 1934, the president of Young Harris College, Jack Lance, conducted the funeral service in the Susan B. Harris Chapel.

Emory Lovick Adams worked and taught at Young Harris College for half a century. He also preached and served as a state legislator. He was responsible for the main road through Young Harris being widened in the early 1950s and the sidewalks built. His marriage to May Sanderson lasted sixty-seven years. Two of their daughters, Mrs. Paul Foster (Marjorie) and Mrs. Lawrence Phillips (Reba), still survive and own some of the original property. The daughter of another daughter (Mary) is Betty Galloway Carringer, whose home on Main Street is also part of the original property of Mrs. Sanderson. She is one of the most loyal of YHC alumni.

William J. "Bud" Miller did marry Jane Melinda Collins in 1886, and they had nine children to add to the six left from Bud's previous marriage. Although Bud did not live to see it, one son, Grady, one daughter, Verdie, and a grandson would become teachers at Young Harris College. Grady was studying at King's College in London, having stayed there after World War I, when he received word that his father, "Bud" Miller, the teacher, had passed away.

There are many descendants of the pioneer Corn families still living in the area, including *Eddie Corn, Cecile Corn Kelley,* and her children: *Mike, Richard, Ann,* and *Doctor John,* who lives in Young Harris in the restored home of his grandparents, Charlie D. and Lydia Dyer Corn. Mr. Corn became the largest landowner in Brasstown Valley and served as mayor for many years.

Another early pioneer family was the Erwins of Brasstown Valley and Choestoe who produced many descendants with connections to Young Harris College. One was the *Reverend George F. Erwin*, class of 1914, who served as a missionary in Siberia, Russia, where he witnessed the Bolshevik Revolution. He also served in Manchuria, China, where he organized seven Methodist churches. After retirement he lived in Upper Hightower, Towns County.

Another prominent member of the family was *Frank Erwin*, longtime principal of Young Harris Grammar School in the 1930s and '40s and taught at Towns County High. His brother *Joseph Sharp Erwin* was my next-door neighbor until his death in 1995. His son, *Charles Erwin*, worked many years for the college, and he and other members of the family still live on Dean Street where the old Erwin homeplaces still stands.

Dr. Thomas Jackson Lance, the Choestoe student who had impressed President Sharp, succeeded him as college president upon his death in 1930 and served as president until 1942. He wrote a beautiful short biography of Dr. Sharp and several informative short histories of the college and Choestoe. *Bert Lance* is the son of *T. Jack Lance* and *Annie Rose Erwin* and presently serves on the Board of Trustees of the college.

Many kin of other early settlers still live in or near Brasstown Valley. It is the magnet that kept them here or drew them back. I have only mentioned a few in this book. There are countless others with stories just as interesting and significant.

Like Haley's Comet, *Byron Herbert Reece* of Choestoe and Young Harris College streaked across the literary sky in the 1940s and '50s. In 1945 his first book of poetry, *Ballad of the Bones*, was published to instant acclaim. Awards and invitations poured in. From coast to coast he was called out of his mountains to meet an adoring public. He won the coveted Guggenheim Fellowship and served as a distinguished lecturer at the University of California and Emory University. In 1950 came his first novel, *Better a Dinner of Herbs*, rapidly followed by *Bow Down in Jericho*, *A Song of Joy*, and *Season of Flesh*. One literary reviewer wrote he "was crowding close upon the literary heels of Sidney Lanier."

In 1955, he published *The Hawk and the Sun* and came back to teach at Young Harris College. But tuberculosis in the family caught up with this frail and sensitive mountain farmer who had a poet's soul. He was in and out of Battey State Hospital, and one June night in 1958 he put one of his favorite pieces of music on the record player and shot himself. He was forty.

For several years a drama, "The Reach of Song," was held each summer and told of the life and times of Reece. Presently an active and enthusiastic Reece Society exists with work underway to commemorate the poet's life with a fitting memorial on the old Reece homeplace near Vogel State Park.

In 1989, the state of Georgia purchased 503 acres of farmland in Brasstown Valley from C. D. Corn, Jr., the great-great-grandson of the Reverend Alfred Corn. A $24.7 million resort, rustic yet luxurious, was built and opened as a public-private relationship in April 1995 as *Brasstown Valley Resort.* The state was required to gather input from the Cherokees and the Council on American Indian Concerns, and careful supervised excavation was made over five acres along Brasstown Creek. Approximately forty burial sites were left undisturbed.

The *Logan Turnpike*, in existence for sixty-two years, was abandoned in 1922 when work was completed on a road across *Neels Gap.* But not before some cars, charged 50 cents each, managed to come through. The current *Richard Russell Scenic Highway* follows much of the same route of the old turnpike on the Union County side.

The landscape of Towns County was changed forever in 1941 when the Tennessee Valley Authority built *Chatuge Dam* across the Hiawassee River. Thirty-five hundred acres of the county's richest farm land went underwater along with 3,500 acres in Clay County, North Carolina. Churches and schools were moved and many families displaced. But electricity, with all its marvelous benefits, came and there was a tremendous boost to the area's economy.

In 2000, the *United Methodist Church* had churches in 396 of 406 Appalachian counties and was the third largest of all denominations in Appalachia, according to the *Encyclopedia of Appalachia.* Of the 11 million United Methodists in the United States, almost 16 percent live in Appalachia.

Young Harris College, more than 120 years after those seven students met in the vacant store, is today an institution with high academic standards and superior teaching. With an enrollment of more than 600 students, its average class size is only 17. More than 70 percent of its faculty hold the doctorate or the highest degree in their field. Its endowment of $110 million makes it one of the best-endowed small private colleges in the Southeast.

The physical plant is valued at more than $41 million with a 30-acre main campus, three academic buildings, a fitness center, Christian life center, gymnasium, dining hall, the Susan B. Harris Chapel, Sharp Memorial United Methodist Church, student center, administrative building, seven residence halls, and five athletic fields. Also available are a six-lane pool, an observatory, a 110-seat planetarium (the third largest in Georgia), and an Outdoor Education building.

The Duckworth Libraries contain 40,000 volumes, 27,000 electronic books, 2,000 microfilm or microfiche, and 1,300 video recordings, and they subscribe to 150 periodicals. Students also have access to hundreds of other databases using GALILEO, the statewide indexing and full text resource.

Approximately 95 percent of Young Harris College students receive some form of scholarship, grant, or work assistance.

Intercollegiate sports include men's baseball and soccer and women's tennis, softball, and soccer. Recently added were men's and women's golf and cross-country.

In April 2007, the Board of Trustees voted unanimously to convert the school to a four-year college offering baccalaureate degrees in subjects yet to be determined, and so the miracle of Brasstown Valley continues.

Acknowledgments

Many who unwittingly contributed to this book are long gone from this valley. But their stories still echo in that lad's ears who once sat spellbound at the "loafer's benches," listening to them spin their tales and make persons he never knew come alive.

Young Harris College and my life are entangled like honeysuckle in an old fence. I was born and reared in its shadow; my father, mother, and an aunt taught in its classrooms. I attended both high school and college there and served on its faculty. It is a major part of what I was and am.

Director of the Duckworth Memorial Library Dawn Lamade and Archivist Debra March were patient and helpful in finding me material that I did not know existed. I am very deeply grateful to both these scholars but hasten to add that any errors in this book are mine and mine alone.

Jerry Taylor is the premier Towns County historian. His knowledgeable suggestions and the fine book he edited, *Hearthstones of Home*, were indispensable. Byron McCombs and Robert Morris were also helpful. Without doubt, the most important primary source was a letter written to the late Jane Akins, Director of Alumni Affairs in 1980, from the grandson of Artemas Lester, Dr. William Marvin Lester, a prominent obstetrician on the medical staff at Emory University and Georgia Baptist hospitals. Dr. Lester, who died in June 2004, also served in the U.S. Navy Medical Corps and was with the Marines at Iwo Jima in World War II. He was survived by his wife of fifty-seven years, Mary Elizabeth Rose Lester, a son, and two daughters.

Other useful sources I enjoyed reading include *History of Young Harris College* (1938) by Joseph Brogdon; *Centennial Chronicle*, a superb little book by Louisa Franklin and Jeffrey Moody; *Sketches of Union County* by C. R. Collins and Jan H. Devereaux, and another volume by Teddy J. Oliver; the great, old classic *Blood Mountain* by Edward L. Shuler; *A History of Northeast Georgia* by Gordon Sawyer;

Mountain Tops by Joseph Bascom Henson; *Living on the Unicoi Road* by Matt Gedney; *The Splendor of Brasstown Valley* by Leota Hunter Hamilton; and the excellent works of Thomas Jackson Lance on Choestoe and Young Harris College. Especially worth reading is his sensitive biography, *Joseph Astor Sharp*, from which I got much information.

I also want to mention the late Dr. E. Merton Coulter, eminent historian and longtime chairman of the Department of History at the University of Georgia. I took every course he taught back in the 1950s and refer to his many books on Georgia history often.

A very special thanks to Heather Wimpy, who typed this manuscript from my hard-to-read longhand. My daughter-in-law, Susan, helped with the photographs, and grandchildren Asia, Andrew, and Bryan helped their Gramp use the Google Internet search engine. Also very helpful was my sister Jane, widow of William Ross, one of the Coker descendants, who as a little girl wrote to Dr. Sharp in the hospital and got back a tender handwritten reply. And last, but far from least, the patient, understanding, indefatigable Shirley Carver Miller, my part-Cherokee wife, who has been propping me up and putting me down as needed and making me look better than I am for more than fifty-three years.

Printed in the United States
148872LV00004BB/18/P